DAVE'S WORLD

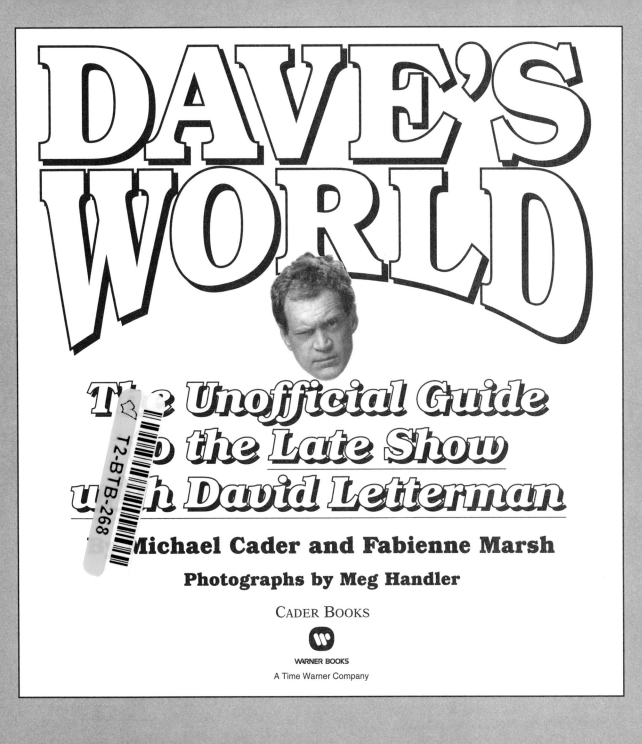

The Unofficial Guide to the Late Show with David Letterman

Michael Cader and Fabienne Marsh

Photographs by Meg Handler

CADER BOOKS

WARNER BOOKS

A Time Warner Company

DAVE'S WORLD

Cover and book design: Charles Kreloff
Cover photographs: Index Stock; Christopher Little/Outline
Warner Books, Inc., 1271 Avenue of the Americas, New York, NY 10020

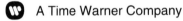 A Time Warner Company

Printed in the United States of America

First printing: January 1995

10 9 8 7 6 5 4 3 2 1

Library of Congress Cataloging-in-Publication Data

Cader, Michael, 1961-
Dave's world : the unofficial guide to the Late show with David Letterman/Michael Cader.
p. cm.
ISBN 0-446-67129-0
1. Letterman, David—Miscellanea. 2. Late show with David Letterman. I. Title.
PN1992.4.L39C34 1995   94-35399
791.45'72—dc20   CIP

Contents

Hello There!

Hi, I'm Michael. your so-called author. Now, where is Dave, your host, you may be asking. Dave couldn't make it—as you can imagine, he's been awfully busy working on the big show, and now that he's trying to drive within the speed limit, it doesn't leave him a lot of time for writing books. Besides, as we know, Dave has all the money. In fact, when Phil Donahue asked him if he was going to write a book he said, "I see no point in that. I'm not sure I would even read that book."

So we took it upon ourselves to write a book for Dave, one that would have that same tasty Dave flavor, and one that might tell us a little more about Dave the man. We learned a lot of things about Dave along the way. What he drives, what he smokes, how his planetary alignments affect his behavior and whether a Guy in a Bear Suit could get into his office.

In the course of researching this book, we naturally read most of Dave's prior interviews. Like most of us, Dave has always been a little nervous about how he is portrayed in print. "Please don't make me look like a dweeb in this. I can tell from your line of questioning and your tone of voice that you're making me out to be a total fucking dweeb. You're not exactly dealing with a chimp here." That's the kind of thing Dave might have just as well said to us.

But like you, our gentle reader, we love Dave. We didn't want to publish anything that would needlessly invade his privacy and we certainly didn't want to make him look like a dweeb. We learned some things that seemed just too per-

sonal, so we are not sharing them with you in this book. But of course Dave has a frequent tendency to discuss some of his own foibles and idiosyncracies with us, the American viewing public, and so we helped ourselves with those and similar subjects. But enough preamble.

We have a great book for you today folks, a terrific piece of reading matter. Please stay tuned.

Dave Says:

"I just don't want to look like a ninny. You're going to make me look like a complete ninny, aren't you? … I just think it's man's natural, primordial fear, coming off like a twit or a ninny."

A Hearty Thank You

Thanks are owed first and foremost to Fabienne Marsh, our chief interrogator, for doing all the hard digging and prodding that made this book possible, and to Meg Handler, who diligently and creatively searched out other people's photographs as well as doing a fine job with her original photography. Walt Chrynwksi, our studio photographer, set a new standard in canned ham portraiture. Charles Kreloff is the one who pulled it all together and made it look great, practically overnight.

A lot of people very kindly put up with a lot of stupid questions and requests from us and we are grateful to them all. We would like to thank Dave in particular, for gently tolerating our uninvited appearances in various corners of his life, and Rosemary Keenan and Dana McClintock, for their patience, understanding, and we suspect, inadvertent assistance. The people in the photo department at CBS were also very kind in working above and beyond the call.

We are very grateful to all of those who consented to be interviewed for this book, and were kind enough to play along with the spirit of the book. Many people were extremely helpful in providing us with information and resources, and anyone with whom we spoke is credited in the book itself. The following people were particularly helpful in supplying visual materials, background information and odd facts, and shared generously of their time: Nick Meglin, MAD Magazine; the Westchester County Police; the Connecticut Police; Dave Schwartz, U.S.G.S., Earthquake Division; Bill Harkness, U.S.G.S., Rivermaster; Danny Epstein; Don Chiodo, U.S. Treasury, Gary Owens; Nelson Price, Indianapolis News; Julian, Marthe and Todd Krainin; Susan Shields, Variety; Deb Hudson, Ball State University; Sidney Maurer.

Everyone at Warner Books has been enthusiastic and supportive from the first mention of this idea, and Mel Parker and Mauro Di Preta in particular have helped to shepherd the project through. We are very appreciative of Alexis Quinlan's unique contribution and of Steve Arenholz's invaluable help at the keyboard and behind the bear's mask.

Special thanks go to Lisa and Jonah, for tolerating a slave to Dave in the house. And to Renee Schwartz for her helpful counsel, and Helene Godin for her informal consultation.

The Nice Folks Who Lent Us Their Pictures

Life and Times

A Dave Timeline

1947

April 12: It's a boy! David Michael Letterman is born in Indianapolis. Dave is a middle child; his sisters are Gretchen and Janice.

Dave Says:

"I can't sing, dance, or act. What else would I be but a talk-show host?"

LATE 1950s

Dave makes his way through P.S. 55.

1961–1965

Dave attends Broad Ripple High School, Indianapolis and is, by all accounts, a mediocre student. Drama teacher Gene Poston clarifies: "He never did fail a subject...He did

"I look like somebody that you would later find out was John Hinckley's best friend or something like that."

enough—the grades were not always indicative of what he got out of the classwork. It's true."

In a rare tour of duty on the side of authority, Dave serves as a hall monitor. "I take exception [with the] claim I was a fink. The hall monitor, at least at Broad Ripple—these were people—we took these positions just to get out of any

organized classroom activity. We could go sit in a darkened hallway and doze or whatever. We didn't fink.... It was just a short vacation."

Jane Pauley attended the same noble institution, as did Marilyn Quayle, class of '67, who recalled, "I didn't like him when I went to school.... Most of the girls in high school didn't like him. He was not a very nice young man."

Dave Says:

"I wasn't the class clown at Broad Ripple High School.... I was the guy who wrote material for the class clown. I dreamed up his stunts, and then when he got arrested, I had a good laugh and went home."

A Dave Timeline

1965

Dave slips into Ball State University in Muncie, Indiana. A radio/TV major, he will join Sigma Chi and meet his first wife, Michelle Cook, a music major.

The Sigma Chi frat house, home to Dave's brothers.

1967

Dave's career begins in earnest, as he works the noon to three P.M. slot on student radio station WBST, a 10-watt powerhouse. The station plays primarily classical music, and Dave can't manage to show the proper on-air decorum, even at this tender age. University officials are reported to be particularly upset when he introduces *Clair de Lune* by remarking, "You remember the De Lune sisters.

There was Clair, there was Mabel." Dave is soon relieved of his $1.25-an-hour post by program director, John Eiden.

WBST now broadcasts a wider variety of programming, including news, different formats of music, and *The Nineteenth State*, a radio documentary about Indiana.

Dave at the controls in his first professional gig, complete with a beaver wrapped around his chin. Oh, wait, that's a beard.

Dave moves on, joining. uh, pirate radio station WAGO, broadcast from a broom closet in the men's dorm, with five watts of power.

Dave (center) flashes a winning smile for the college yearbook.

Dave Says:

"I used to have a radio program on WBST and that was just the best. That was my first outlet, my first place to just go and talk, and I loved it."

Sacker, Stocker, Supermarket Guy

Sidney Maurer (center) and the current staff of Atlas Supermarket pose outside of the store, by a billboard honoring their former employee.

High school wasn't all fun and pranks for Dave. He worked for a number of years for Sidney Maurer, owner of the Atlas Supermarket, who gave Dave his first job. Dave has said in the past, "It was the market of choice. It wasn't just a job, it was a step in social maturation. To this day the Atlas experience remains one of the most positive influences in my life. It was the first time I was entrusted with real responsibility." So we caught up with Sid Maurer to find out more about this formative experience.

How did Dave do at his job?
David had the ability to absorb what we were teaching and go further with it. In other words when we would teach him the

A front view of Atlas—nice people, nice prices!

Dave Says:
"I'm very resourceful. I'd be good in prison. I'd be good in a shipwreck. I'd make a great hostage. Oh, I have talents aplenty. Unfortunately, precious few of them have any redeeming social value."

bagging, we would teach him how to talk with people, we would teach him about responsibility and as he absorbed, then we would see the development and bring him up another notch. He went from sacking to stocking and went from stocking to learning how to run a register and then, being dependable and driving, he took on responsibility and just kept going on up.

Was Dave particularly skilled at anything?
We're limited in what skills we can actually see. The sacking he was very good at, which means eyeball coordination to take what goes into a bag and pack it in there and get it in the right spot. It's very difficult to be a really good sacker.

Dave has told stories about pilfering groceries when he worked for you. Are you aware of this? He always talks about the deal about stashing beer in the dumpster. I seriously doubt if that ever happened in the store. I don't want to dispute him, okay? I just turn my head the other way and forget about it.

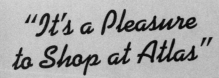

"It's a Pleasure to Shop at Atlas"

To give us a taste of the shopping experience, the folks at Atlas supermarket kindly prepared this list of slogans used in the store over the years:

No Coupons—No Gimmicks

It's a Pleasure to Shop at Atlas

Hard to Get Items Are Easy to Find at Atlas

Indy's Truly One of a Kind Supermarket

No One Has More Items than Atlas

Indy's Leading Gourmet Supermarket

Indy's Oldest Independent Supermarket and Still Growing

Good Wines Don't Have to Be Expensive.

(Deli Motto)
Taste N' Try Before You Buy

A small selection of some of the fine and plentiful grocery items available at the Atlas Market, "the market of choice," according to Dave.

What were the staples of the Letterman household back then?
I hate to tell you this, but I am one supermarket grocery operator who never looks at the cart. In other words, you'll never ever have me run an ad where you have to buy five or ten dollars worth of stuff in order to get a price. We don't use coupons—you don't have to have a coupon to walk in and get a sale item.

Would you hire Dave again now? If he needed a job, would you take him back?
If things ever got bad, which is ridiculous to think, if he wanted to come work for me anytime, yes, I would hire him…. But it's [really] just a stepping-stone to go into their next job.

But if he really needed a break, you'd take him back.
David is a good soul. Let's put it this way and I have never told this to anybody, I'm not sure I should. My wife and I bought a house [back when Dave was working at the store] and Dave volunteered to help. We loaded up the car and

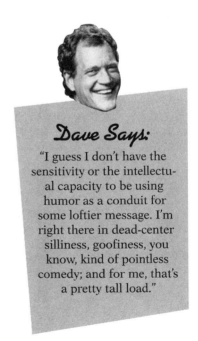

Dave Says:

"I'm the kind of guy that on a hot day, if a neighbor comes over and needs help installing a through-the-window air conditioner …
I'll be there."

stuff and he brought it to the house and we helped unload it and so forth. But he would do that if his next-door neighbor was going to be putting a window air conditioner or something and he noticed it—he'd go over and ask if he could help.

If you were to write a letter of recommendation for David, what would it say?
That David is a down to earth, hard working, caring person, completely trustworthy, and anyone who gets him to work for them can relax because whatever he'll do, he'll do it as best he possibly can and try to improve on what he does.

In your professional opinion, if Dave hadn't gone on to broadcasting, do you think he had the makings of a career grocer?
It's like in any kind of a puzzle, if the pieces fit the right way, yes, he would do good. But the grocery business is different than most any other business—it's a heavily people business, similar to what Dave is doing now, but it's also something where you have to have the luck and go....

Dave would have had the right stuff if he had elected to stay in it. But he didn't.

What was the deal with Dave's hair back when he worked for you?
It didn't break any rules where it was down to his shoulders, do you know what I mean? At the time that he was in here, David's hair was the usual standard haircut type thing, not wavy, not a finger running through your hair type thing. I don't think he quite had a style.

Dave Says:

"I guess I don't have the sensitivity or the intellectual capacity to be using humor as a conduit for some loftier message. I'm right there in dead-center silliness, goofiness, you know, kind of pointless comedy; and for me, that's a pretty tall load."

Could a Guy in a Bear Suit Get into Dave's Office?

Guy in a Bear Suit arrives at the entrance to Dave's office building.

He's going in.

Doorman Kendall objects to taking pictures of a Guy in a Bear Suit.

Guy in a Bear Suit tries reasoning with Kendall. Kendall agrees to call up to Dave's office, but insists that Guy in a Bear Suit wait out by the curb, so as not to interfere with other business.

Guy in a Bear Suit is escorted out, unable to get into Dave's office.

Guy in a Bear Suit continues to wait patiently for Dave's answer. Kendall takes the photographer in to speak to Dave's publicist on the telephone.

Guy in a Bear Suit consoles himself outside of Hello Deli.

Dave's Mater

Darrell Wible, a professor in the Telecommunications Department at Ball State, was Dave's mentor in college. "You never know how talent will evolve or be recognized. I couldn't have predicted his spectacular success, but I remember walking down the hallway with a faculty member who said, 'That Letterman is stupid.'

"I said, 'As far as I'm concerned, David Letterman is a creative genius.'"

College pal Jeffrey Lewis has had this to say: "No, he was not popular with the girls. He had one steady girlfriend and he wasn't popular with her."

A lovely aerial shot of the Ball State campus today, located in scenic Muncie, Indiana.

Letterman Scholarship

Ever since Dave made it big he has been kind enough to share the wealth. In fact, a number of people we spoke to told us of Dave's many charitable contributions to people, organizations, and institutions in his native state of Indiana, often made anonymously through friends and a local attorney. One well-known beneficiary of Dave's generosity is the Letterman Scholarship, available to juniors in the Telecommunications Department at Ball State University since 1985. The grant is used toward tuition, housing, room and board for the student's senior year. (Prospective applicants should note carefully that only Ball State students are eligible.) The scholarship is available to all applicants, regardless of their academic record. Winners are selected by a panel of professors and students from the Telecommunications Department. Dave does not participate in selecting the winners, though he does receive materials from the applicants, and has often contributed additional funds to support more students than originally intended. Last year's grants provided $8,570 to the first-place student, $4,285 to the second-place student, and $2,856 to the third-place student.

Ball State officials have asked us to clear up the misconception that the scholarship is specif-ically limited to C students. Dave did, however, donate $25,000 for a production room for the department. That room is dedicated to C students, but is also available for use by more accomplished pupils.

Wes Gehring, a professor of film in the Telecommunications department, is the current liaison for the Letterman Fellowship. His specialty is American film comedy, and his ninth book, a critical look at Groucho Marx and W.C. Fields as huckster figures, will be published this fall.

We spoke to him about the fellowship, and about Dave's college days.

The plaque that commemorates the telecommunications production room donated by grateful alum, Dave.

THE LETTERMAN FELLOWS: WHERE ARE THEY NOW?

"Probably the most prominent person is Thomas Gulley. He runs his own advertising firm in Indianapolis and has won a number of—I forget what the award's called now, it's kind of the local version of the Emmy in terms of advertising. He's been the most prominent. A number of them have gone out and are working in Hollywood for a number of different production companies. Nobody has really gone on to huge fame and fortune."

THE TYPICAL SUBMISSION

"The typical entry that we get is a video of about fifteen minutes in length, but we've had winners that have done everything from screenplays to compose music, to doing radio programs. We even had one year a student who did a really elaborate storyboard for a film but the most typical entry is a 15-minute video."

ADVICE FOR APPLICANTS

"The thing we always try to encourage—and I think Letterman wanted to do it in the first place—was to just give students a reason why they're here. To make something that means a lot to them and ideally something that they can use later on as an example of 'what I can' do when they go out on a job interview. The advice would be to personalize it as much as you can in terms of it being something that represents you but at the same time, look for something that's a mainstream."

DAVE'S HAIR AS A STUDENT

I've seen some old footage when he used to work as a weatherman out of Indianapolis. It was just sort of longer and sort of puffish, you know I'm not saying a Beatles cut but there was a lot more hair there.

FORMER WINNERS

Thomas Gulley, Carmel
Winner, 1985-86, $5,015.00
"Jake Stone - Private Eye"

Rich Swingley, Muncie
2nd, 1985-86, $3,000.00
"Party Animal"

Rich Swingley, Muncie
Winner, 1986-87, $5,235.00
"You Can Always Find A Way"

Mark Racop, Logansport
2nd, 1986-87, $2,600.00
"Eyes of the Cat"

A Dave Timeline

ALL STATE UNIVERSITY   MUNCIE, INDIANA 47306

THE CENTER FOR RADIO AND TELEVISION

David M. Letterman
2024 W. Main St.
Muncie, Indiana
January 26, 1969

Mr. Gary Owens
KMPC Los Angeles

Dear Mr. Owens:

I am a senior in college and I have spent the last three years in the field of commercial broadcasting, working and studying. While I enjoy, and find challenge in broadcasting, I have come to realize that is only because it gives me an opportunity to use material which I have written myself. I would enjoy a career in radio and television only if it would involve creative writing; more specifically, comedy.

The problem is, however, that I don't know how to get a job as a writer. I have had several occasions to perform my material successfully, but unfortunately I don't pay myself to write jokes. When I graduate in June, I have a job waiting in Indianapolis with the ABC Television affiliate, where I have worked for the last two summers as a booth announcer and weekend weatherman. "Hot Diggity", you may be saying to yourself by now, but I would rather be a writer.

As mentioned above, I am completely ignorant as to what to do to prepare myself for a writing career, of even what to do to secure one. If you have the time, I would greatly appreciate any advice or suggestions you could give. Thank you very much for yourtime and trouble.

Sincerely,
David Letterman

Would-be mentor Gary Owens

Preparing for the cruel world ahead, Dave seeks professional counsel from those who know best, including Gary Owens at KMPO in Los Angeles, whom he writes to for career advice.

1970

Dave graduates, barely, from Ball State.

Off to fulfull his dreams, Dave begins his professional career at WERK, a local radio station. As he told Phil Donahue, "I wanted to be a broadcaster. I wanted to work at WLW in Cincinnati. It's a clear channel, 50,000 watt radio station, and it used to boom in Indianapolis. They produced a lot of really good broadcasting talent in that area and that's what I wanted to do is be a disc jockey at a radio station like that. I went to college and ended up doing television. And after about five years I got very tired of it because I wasn't getting anywhere."

Dave then makes the move to the tube. He joins WLWI-TV (Channel 13, now called WTHR) in Indianapolis. He hosts a late-night movie show that comes on at 2 A.M. which he names *Freeze-Dried Movies*, and *Clover Power*, a Saturday morning program that showcases local kids in the 4-H Club. He also sits in as weatherman on the news.

1975

Michelle and David Letterman arrive in Los Angeles.

Dave gives stand-up a try, opening at Mitzi Shore's Comedy Store, where Jay Leno catches his act. Dave is hired as a regular.

A Dave Timeline

Jimmie "Dyn-o-mite" Walker

Jimmie Walker, starring as J.J. in the sitcom, *Good Times*, hires Dave to write 15 jokes a week for $150. "He wanted me to write jokes with a black point of view. He was the first black person I had ever seen."

1977

Michelle Cook and David Letterman divorce.

Dave's writing for *The Paul Lynde Comedy Hour*.

Dave makes a number of significant TV guest spots beginning this year, including a week on *The Gong Show* (July 4–8), a spot as a celebrity contestant for a week on *The Twenty-Thousand Dollar Pyramid*, and an appearance on *Mork and Mindy*, in which he plays the mean-spirited leader of the ERK (Ellsworth Revitalization Konditioning) Group.

Dave, the hardest-working young man in show business, joined Chuck Barris for a full week on The Gong Show.

Big-time stars of song and small screen Jon, Margot, Taffy, and Bill of The Starland Vocal Band. They gave Dave his first regular television slot.

Hey kids, do you like the rock and roll? The Starland Vocal Band's smash hit, "Afternoon Delight," leads to a comedy and variety show on CBS in the summer. Dave joins the show as a writer, announcer, and performer.

Dave Says:

"I originally went to Los Angeles as a writer. It's more palatable to tell your family that you're going to be a writer than it is to tell them that you're going to do stand-up comedy. They think you're looking for circus work or something like that."

A Dave Timeline

1978

Dave appears in a number of specials this year, including *Celebrity Cooks, Battle of the Network Stars V,* and *Peeping Times*. (A secretary in the *Peeping Times* office tells Dave he needs to get his teeth fixed.)

A bushy-haired Dave proudly wears the CBS colors as he competes in Battle of the Network Stars V.

Dave lands a role in the ill-fated comedy variety show *Mary*, starring Mary Tyler Moore and featuring such regulars as Dick Shawn, Swoosie Kurtz, and Michael Keaton. The show is canceled after three weeks, but

The Letterman Forecast:

"Nothing is going to happen to us as far as weather is concerned. It's going to be just like it was yesterday, and just like it is today, and it's going to be like that tomorrow and again on Tuesday, because nothing's going on."

"Indiana at one time yesterday. But all of that seems of little importance once you take a look at the cloud cover photograph made earlier of the United States today, and I think you'll see that once again we have fallen to the prey of political dirty dealings. The higher-ups have removed the border between Indiana and Ohio, making it one giant state. Personally, I'm against it."

It's hard to find a verifiable picture of Dave in his weatherman days, but he certainly looks like a weatherman in this picture. He's said of himself in that period, "Looked like one of the Monkees, didn't I?"

"I made up my own measurements for hail and said that hailstones the size of canned hams were falling."

A Dave Timeline

Dave strikes up a relationship with one of television's all-time greats. Unfortunately, the show folds after three weeks on the air. Dave commented, "It was pretty exciting, having heard about Television City all my life, to be going to work there. I had

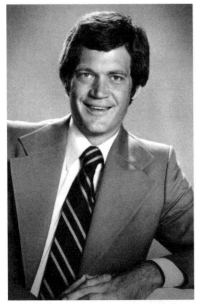

Dave's publicity picture while a cast member of Mary, *which aired for only three weeks. The Letterman smile just doesn't seem the same here, and it's not because of the contrasting lapels. A close look reveals that the trademark gap is missing from Dave's smile, due to a temporary dental insert.*

a name badge with a picture on it and an ID number, and I could eat in the CBS commissary. I could talk to Mary Tyler Moore anytime I wanted. I could do almost anything. I could share fruit with her if I wanted to. I, of course, wanted to. She never wanted any part of it.

"But the hard part was that I had to sing and dance and dress up in costumes. That was tough. I knew my limitations, but this really brought them home. You know, it was, 'You're not a singer. You're not a dancer. You're not an actor. Get out of here. What are you doing? Get away from Mary. That's her fruit. Don't try and eat that fruit.'"

Johnny Carson's staff catches Dave on *Mary*, and on Novem-

Dave in his first Tonight Show *appearance. He was invited to sit with Johnny, but here he doesn't quite look ready to be at the King's side.*

ber 24 he appears on the *Tonight Show* and talks with the master himself.

1979

Is that Dave playing Matt Morgan in the TV movie *Fast Friends*? You bet.

In April NBC offers Letterman a two-year contract for a show with the working title, *Leave It To Dave*. "The whole project

A Dave Timeline

was just a disaster from Word One. I was supposed to sit on a throne, and the set was all pyramids. The walls were all covered in shag carpet. It was like some odd Egyptian theme sale at Carpeteria.

"At one point I was in New York, and I got a phone call from the West Coast. They said, 'We've come up with a great idea. Your guests will all sit around on pillows.' And I hung up the phone and I turned to my manager, Jack Rollins, and I said, 'This moron wants us to sit on pillows. What's the mat-

Wake up, kids! It's Dave on the first day of his morning show, with not one but two models of the Statue of Liberty. How could Mujibur and Sirajul have known?

Dave works the crowd at a gig in 1979. Groovy pants, Dave.

ter with chairs?' You could just see the elements kind of—I hate to say it was like dominoes toppling, but it was like dominoes toppling."

Dave films an HBO special, *David Letterman: Looking for Fun.* HBO now has this one sealed away in a vault.

1980

On June 23, *The David Letterman Show* airs. Stupid Pet Tricks make their first appearance on this show. Good news: the show wins two Emmys. Bad news: it's canceled in September. Dave returns to California, still under contract to NBC.

31

A Dave Timeline

1982

On February 1 *Late Night with David Letterman* premieres on NBC at 12:30 A.M. The first celebrity guest is Bill Murray, who sings "Let's Get Physical."

Dave welcomes America to the first episode of Late Night with David Letterman. *The tie still needs some work.*

1984

In September Dave's Mom remarries.

1988

On May 22 Margaret Ray is stopped at the Lincoln Tunnel tollbooth, on the New Jersey side, driving Dave's car and claiming to be his wife. This is the first of many Margaret Ray run-ins in Dave's life. She will later claim to be his housekeeper, rake leaves on his tennis court, and do laundry in his swimming pool.

On August 22 Dave's beloved German Shepard, Bob, dies. "It turned out Bob was ridden with cancer. He had eaten a Presto log and as a result, his lungs were covered with tumors. But they give off a nicely colored flame if burned—very festive for the holidays. So [Merrill Markoe] called and said the vet thought we should put him to sleep. I said I'd be off the following week and would come out. But the vet said we couldn't wait. So they put him to sleep right there, which was—it was sad."

1993

On August 30 New Dave is born, as *Late Show with David Letterman* premieres on CBS, from the Ed Sullivan Theater, featuring guests NEXIS CHECK.

Dave Says:

Dave once suggested the following as his epitaph: "David Letterman. He wasn't funny, but he wasn't an asshole."

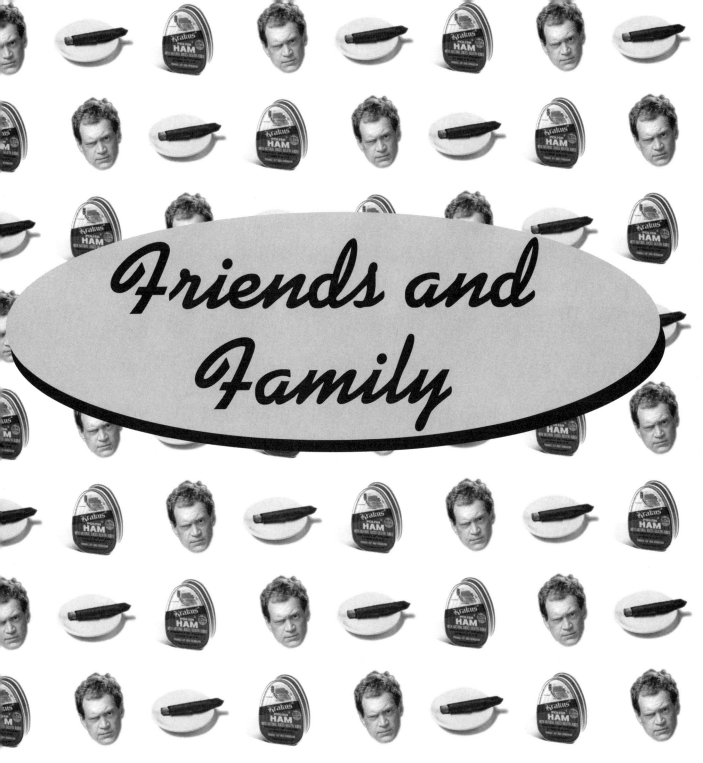

Friends and Family

Meet the Family

Dave comes from true, hardworking, hearty American stock. Both of his grandfathers were miners who later became farmers. Here are photographic conceptions of what Dave's grandpas might have looked like. Clearly, cap wearing is an old family tradition.

We hear—and see—a lot of Dave's mom. Dave's dad, Joseph Letterman, passed on at age 57, in 1973. He was a florist, who had the first FTD franchise in Indianapolis, and served as an FTD director from 1962–1965.

Dave's mom, chatting with Hillary Rodham Clinton at the Lillehammer Olympics, in a futile attempt to get presidential intervention on her son's speeding tickets. Now retired, except for her freelance television work, Mom was secretary of the Second Presbyterian Church for 16 years. She remarried after Dave's dad passed on, so her last name is no longer Letterman. Her married name has been kept private and we're told that she is considering legally changing her name to Dave's Mom.

Dave Says:

"I see this in my mother: She is the least demonstrative person I've ever been around. I feel like if you can notice that with her, by virtue of genetics you're going to notice that with me. Her countenance will reveal no interest, no stimuli, no rsponse, nothing. Then you ask her about it and she gets angry because, of course, she is paying rapt attention and is following the conversation."

SHRINKING DAVE

Dave's a swell guy, but sometimes we worry about him. After all, he's in his late forties and has been single for years. He thrives on driving fast and ignoring the authorities, he's always bringing his mother along, he clearly needs public approval, and although he seems much happier this past year, he's been known to be a little tetchy with guests. We sought some professional advice on Dave's behalf, consulting with Dr. Mark S. Goulston, assistant clinical professor of psychiatry at the UCLA Neuropsychiatric Institute. Not only that, he's been on *Oprah*. Throughout the book we'll be featuring excerpts from our interview with Dr. Goulston on particular topics of interest.

Does Dave like women?
He likes women, but probably could never find one that would get the seal of approval from his two sisters and mother, i.e., any woman would have three strikes on her before she came to bat.

What role does Johnny Carson play in Dave's life?
Johnny Carson is a father figure for Dave, but he's frustrated that his signature gesture of making a fist and a punching motion backed up by Paul Shaffer's drummer is not as powerful as Johnny's signature golf swing that he used at the end of his dialogues.

Dave has two sisters and he's a middle child. In light of this, is any of his behavior "textbook"?
When you're a middle child of like sexes, typically you're not as respected as your older sibling and not as "cute" as your younger sibling, and therefore not as likely to get away with impudence. But if you're the only male in between two females, your specialness is guaranteed. So in Dave's case, the specialness of being the only boy compensates for his middle and therefore ignorable status. That he cross-dresses is mere coincidence.

Dave is in his late forties, has no children, and is not married. Is there a problem here?
The main problem for Dave—being in his late forties, being un-married and with no children—is dealing with all the envy of men in their late forties who are married and who have children.

Dave Says:
"I have a very low threshold of self-embarrassment."

Dave, Jr.?

A lot of Dave's fans worry about him. Will we ever see Dave's spitting image spitting on his knee? Does Dave even have family urges? A couple of years ago the scenario seemed pretty grim, but with the new improved Happy Dave, everything's looking a bit different.

Dave does have a steady girlfriend, but out of respect, we're not going to tell you her name or her job, or that her family is from Ohio, and we're not going to show you the picture that we have of her jogging—which wasn't a very good picture anyway and would have set us back 100 big ones.

But we are given to understand that Dave does know life is passing him by and he'd better get started on a family soon. Here's what he said last year on the subject: "I get very excited about kids. A while back, all of my friends started having kids, and I was spending more time with infants than I had ever spent since I was an infant. And I found them just a wonder. It was something that I hadn't really thought about until the last two or three years. So I've decided that as soon as I get everything in my life just perfect, then I'll start having kids. I'm looking at maybe six, eight months of fine-tuning, and then we're on to the family."

Dave Says:

"I'm a wise-ass and a smart ass, and I always have been."

SHRINKING DAVE

Does Dave love his mother?
He loves his mother, but is frustrated that he can take her out of the country, but can't take the country out of her. She's also his toughest audience. C'mon, Dave, lighten up! Just because she doesn't get it, doesn't mean you're not funny. You'll just never be as funny as her not getting it.

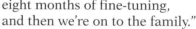

UH, DAVE, I WAS WONDERING WHERE YOU GOT THAT WACKY LAST NAME...

From an appearance by Dave on the Donahue *show:*

VIEWER: First of all, your last name really strikes me. I was wondering if it had anything to do with the postal service in your hometown?

LETTERMAN: No.

(Dave does claim to receive mail every day from the woman who broke into his house, though.)

Could a Guy in a Bear Suit Get into the New Today Show Studio?

Guy in a Bear Suit surveys the scene.

Anybody home?

Despite the warm welcome, a Guy in a Bear Suit is not allowed into the studio, unless he is already booked for the program.

We have contact!

Guy in a Bear Suit is consoled by the larger-than-life image of Katie.

Howdy Neighbor!

It's no secret that Broadway between 53rd and 54th streets was a fairly nondescript part of the fine city of New York before CBS renovated the Ed Sullivan Theater and installed Dave inside. Since that momentous occasion, Dave and his neighbors have become true friends, appearing at each other's place of business, stopping for friendly chats, and so forth. We, the American viewing public, have come to know these upstanding businesspeople as Dave has met them and welcomed them into his life.

We wanted to know a little bit more about a few of these interesting folks, who you will encounter in the following pages. Here is a brief Letterman Phone Book to help you contact the members of Dave's own little Chamber of Wacky Commerce.

Longacre Copy Center
1691 Broadway
581-7077

Bagel Cafe
1707 Broadway
245-5400

Academy Clothes
1703 Broadway
765-1440

Hello Deli
213 West 53rd Street
489-7832

Flash Dancers
1674 Broadway
315-5107

San-Leone Pizza
1674 Broadway
265-1414

Santino Photo Electronic
1693 Broadway
397-6062

K & L's Rock America
1705 Broadway
757-3926

Mujibur and Sirajul

We see a lot of Dave's new friends and next-door neighbors, Mujibur and Sirajul, but we don't hear a lot from them. We talked to each one individually, to give you a better sense of the two of them as people, and we traveled to Astoria, Queens, to visit them both at home, away from the hustle and bustle of Broadway and K & L's Rock America. Both are married; Mujibur has a fourteen-year-old daughter and a twelve-year-old son; Sirajul has a five-year-old daughter. (They wanted us to make it clear that they only work at Rock America, they don't own the store, which is run by their boss, Kay Lee.)

Let's Visit Mujibur

What part of your journey in this great land of ours did you like best?
The Grand Canyon. The spectacle was amazing and I can feel how God is a superpower, how he can create such a wonderful thing on this earth. I feel that way, and as a goodwill ambassador on the tour, I feel very much comfortable meeting Dave's mom. Because I feel Dave's our very much good friend. He was a tremendous promotion in this country and I feel too much grateful to him and I was really expecting to see his family. So when I see his mom, I feel really great, and she's a wonderful person.

Do Dave and his mother resemble each other in person?
The face is almost look alike. She has her own personality. I feel she's very quiet person and very generous and very kindly.

What was your life like before you met Dave?
Every day when I go home, I would watch the *Charlie Rose* show and I would enjoy it long time. When Charlie Rose moved to PBS, then I quit because it was a different time. Then I started watching the David Letterman show on NBC. I feel like with Dave's show you can have a lot of humor as well you can a lot of good information about this country, about this society, about the personalities of all the celebrities, you know, all the different culture, even in the world. The first half hour of Dave's show, it was really wonderful, the way he start the show. The "Good

Mujibur and Sirajul, in one of their official CBS publicity shots, displaying some of their favorite wares from the store. The one on the left is Mujibur.

Mujibur relaxes at home.

evening, ladies and gentleman, I am Dave, your host." I like this thing.

What was your favorite moment on the show?
When I decorated the Christmas tree. The way people love us, people kidding us, and I decorated and I make a joke with him on the stage. I enjoy that show.

In your career, do you see a way to incorporate your political science and legal training?
I want to work with Dave and I love to work with Dave in entertainment and I love that and I enjoy that, at this moment.

Do you want your own talk show?
No, I don't want that.

How did you come to settle in Astoria?
One of my cousins went to school in the States and he introduced me to his other friend, who used to live in Astoria. I became a roommate of my cousin's friend. His name Jia Uddin Bablo

and still we are very close to each other. I enjoyed the neighborhood and people was very friendly with us. I still live in Astoria.

Do you know a nice Bangladeshi girl to set Dave up with?
Actually, our Bangladeshi woman is very much conservative. Too much conservative. Anyway, I don't get involved in anybody's personal life.

If Dave could go to Bangladesh with you, where would you take him?
I'd take him first to the village where I was born, Palakata, and the hometown Coxbazar. Palakata in Coxbazar; like Astoria in Queens. It's named after one of the British guys in the time of World War I. He was very nice to the people around that neighborhood. Mr. Cox is name. The city's name Coxbazar. It's pretty much western and Coxbazar is one of the most beautiful cities in the Southeast Asian countries. We have a 70-mile-long sea beach. Wonderful beauty.

Beginning morning prayer.   *It's time for work!*

Does Bangladesh have a television star like Dave?
One person, he was very much famous—he died. His name Fazla Lohani. Now another guy his name Hanif. His show similar to the Dave show—interviews, they do talking, they throw out the social problem. I enjoy that part. Like Dave, so many times he talk about the health care plan. This Hanif, he talk about the communication system—he make a laugh. Laughing, you make the point.

Do you think Dave should fix the gap between his teeth?
I have to mention it again—he's my very close friend, my good friend, I don't want to go into personal things.

Is there anything you want to add?
I love all kinds of people, all age of people. I respect them as best, from beginning of my life this is my hobby, to help the people. When I was a student in ninth grade I helped the poor people in my village. When I was going to college, I had a lot of poor student in the college. When I was going to University, I was involved in Sigma Chi Alpha Beta, like one of the most powerful organizations in the country. I was a secretary. One of my roommate was part of the government for the last five years in Bangladesh.

   I love to serve and help the people. When I first came to this country, our country was a martial or military government; so we all pushed the government from here and we have a committee and it's named Committee for Democrats in Bangladesh. One of my uncle, he was member of Parliament, before Bangladesh back it was the Pakistan. He was minister of labor in the whole country, and his name was Farid Ahmed and he was one of the biggest parliamenters in Pakistan.

Let's Visit Sirajul

Relaxing on the subway.

Which part of the trip across America did you like best?
I like personally not the urban area really; I like the natural part of what America has been. Right, Grand Canyon, it is part of America maybe 200 years ago or 2,000 years ago it was in a river or something. And the next one you could say was Niagara Falls, it's the world's largest fall or something, and also the Montana where we were fishing before. That was real nice. All of the ones that are natural, that's what I like best.

You have a master's in Literature. What Bangladeshi authors should Americans be reading?
I'm not prepared that much, but I can tell you right now I like Professor Sokwat Ali; he's a very literate person, genius, good author. Professor Sokwat Ali, he's serious writer, not like easy writer. Another writer, his name Byed Shamsul Haque—before long ago, he was also working at BBC, he is also in Bangladesh like a novel writer. We have two big writers in Bangladesh I have to tell you first this one. One was Tagore, you maybe heard the name. And Rabindranath Tagore, he write lot of song, lot of novel, lot of poetry books, everything—and he got a Nobel prize 1913.

Sirajul in his living room.

Do you have a favorite writer here?
I just read every day newspaper like *New York Times*, sometimes *Daily News*. And I watch TV and *The New York Times* because I have not that much time. But some novel book I read in like paperback. I read some book, like a Danielle Steel. I read some books when I'm walking down the subway.

Is there anyone you really admire in America.
Well, we meet with Tom Jones. He's a nice singer and I love him really, because when we meet with him he's like a very good friend of ours. Like he know long time. So we're very glad that time. Tom Jones is a big artist and he knows us and we meet with him in the MGM Hotel in Las Vegas and stay in apartment with his manager. We just sitting in there and just talking in the lobby. And then the other day we went to his show, the light show in MGM Hotel. After the show he just give us a chance to talk with him and we presented two T-shirt, two hat, and he just offered some of them drinks and like cold drinks and chips. And it's so nice, to talk with us. I love him really.

Is there a David Letterman of Bangladesh?
One guy is Fazla Lohani. He was long time in London with the BBC, so maybe he get idea from there, and he get back to Bangladesh in '71 and he start the show on TV. Like a magazine program, *Jodi Kechu Mona Had Na Koran*, which means, "if you don't mind something, I can tell you."

And what about that gap between Dave's teeth?
I like that, I like that really. This is a nice thing in his face. I don't feel it's ugly. I like that one and it's really nice, and sometimes when it's mentioned like that, that's okay.

I can tell you this thing, David Letterman is a person. He's just blessing for me. He just came out, he just send the camera one day and stopped with me and Mujibur and we went to the stage and frequently he offered us to the stage, and to the show. I'm really grateful to him and he's great really, and God bless him and his family.

Do you have any goals?
I'd like to stick with Dave, with the show. How long time, I don't know. But how long it's possible that I can stay with Dave, I've been thinking like that. If I stick with Dave, it's better for me; and better, I try to do something for the show also, because people love that we are joining the show. Our appearances, they love it. So myself, my duty, I think, or my responsibility to do something more for the show. I don't know how much I can do.

Could a Guy in a Bear Suit Get a Book Deal With Warner Books?

Receptionist insists that Kirshbaum is not in. Guy in a bear suit chooses to wait it out in the comfort of Kirshbaum's office.

Having made it past Time Warner security in the lobby, Guy in a Bear Suit admires the work of his fellow authors while waiting to meet with Warner CEO Laurence Kirshbaum.

Bear gives up, his story still untold.

"Roger, Fern, Do You Copy?"

One of Dave's new friends and neighbors is Fern Chapnick, who runs the Longacre Copy Center, on the northwest corner of Broadway and 53rd street. In the window are her color photocopies of Dave's face.

What was your favorite moment on the show?
The first time he came in, I was in a state of shock and I couldn't believe it. He came in and introduced himself. I think my mouth must have been hanging open. He introduced himself and said, "I'd like you to xerox your face." I looked at him like he was crazy, and said, "Sure, I can do that." He said, "I'll be back for the picture." He walked out and I said to my husband, "He's not coming back. Let's continue working." And my husband said, "No, he'll be back." So sure enough I had to climb on the machine. It was very difficult. I had to climb on the machine and shut off the light because you can't have any light in the background. It has to be covered over. That's for the color machine. The black-and-white machine is no trouble.

Did Dave look different in person?
He's a good-looking man. He's very tall. His hair is better in person—it doesn't look so matted-down—and his features are better in person.

Are his teeth better in person?
No. He has a space between his front teeth. And my brother, being a dentist, I think he should fix his teeth. I think he would do a good job. Any way he was a pleasant person. I was surprised about that. His reputation didn't say to me that he was going to be as nice as he was.

Anything you'd like to add?
Yeah. I'd like to know why it's so darn hard to get tickets. I mean, *really*. I tried for two. I didn't get them. It's the hardest thing to get through to that office. It's unbelievable. I've never had a show like this. I mean, I can get tickets to other shows that I deal with.

Like Cats.
Yes. Andrew Lloyd Webber is one of our clients.

One's a Ham, the Other's Chicken

Rupert Jee at the Hello Deli, directly adjacent to the entrance to Dave's office building on 53rd street, has created sandwiches in honor of Dave and Paul. Can you tell which is which?

THE BIFF
SAUTÉED ROAST BEEF, CHEESE, ONIONS, HOT PEPPERS, TOMATO, LETTUCE, MAYO
STEAK

SHAFFER
KEN CUTLET, TOMATO, CHEESE 40

LETTERMAN
TURKEY, HAM, CHEESE, LETTUCE, TOMATO, SWEET PEPPERS, OIL & VINEGAR
HOAGIE

SPECIAL
TURKEY BURGER
$??

Answer: Paul is on the left (he's cheesier), Dave is on the right (he's cold cuts)

Remember Meg?

Dave's new friends have been getting a lot of attention, so we checked in with one of Dave's best-known old friends from his former neighborhood, Meg Parsont, to see how life after Dave is treating her. She was kind enough to share her memories and opinions with us.

How did Dave first contact you?
My office at Simon & Schuster was directly across from what was then the NBC building. The Letterman offices were really and truly on the exact same level as my office across the street. And one day, around 5:30, the phone rang. I answered it and the guy on the other end said, "Hi. Who am I talking to?" And I hate it when people don't tell me who they are right away. So I got a little bit snippity when I said in my best publicist's voice, "Well, who am *I* speaking with?" And he said it was Dave Letterman in the little nickel-and-dime show across the street. And of course I didn't believe him. I had to believe it was a phony phone call. The only way they got me to believe him is when they told me to look outside my window and I could see all the NBC people in there waving at me.

Ostensibly they were calling to find somebody who was working late that day. And they wanted to award that person the Office Person of the Month Award, which was a really seedy suit of men's clothing. It didn't matter that I was a woman. I did get that suit.

Did Dave ever ask you out on a date?
No.

Would you have gone if he did ask you?
No.

Do you find his hair sexy?
His *hair?* Do I really have to answer this?

Yes.
No. I don't.

In September Dave moved to a new office. In December Meg moved to a new office, shown above. Hmmm.

Do you find his gap sexy?
I don't really find anything sexy about him. I think he seems like a very nice, intelligent man. I don't really look upon him in any way beyond that.

What were your favorite moments?
My favorite was when, for my birthday several years ago, he shut traffic down and sent a marching band down the street playing "Happy Birthday." Once they were under my window they went into formation to spell out my name. The best part, in Dave's mind, was that you could look out my window and see traffic backed up to the East River. I think it gave Dave a certain sense of power.

Another time they had the Harlem Boy's Choir come to my office right before Christmas and sing Christmas carols. And there were about 25 boys ranging from about 8 to 16 in my office. They had the most beautiful voices. And I really almost cried. I think if I hadn't been on air I probably would have cried.

The other time I almost cried is when they had a live turkey brought into my office to commemorate Thanksgiving. Larry "Bud" Melman, as he was known then, was dressed up as a Pilgrim. The turkey was never going to be killed. It was a live turkey who makes live appearances — but I was so worried he was going to hurt himself that I started getting a little flustered. He was flapping his wings on my desk.

Do you have any favorite moments from the new show?
To tell the truth, I don't really watch it very frequently. I guess I watch it a little more often now that it's on an hour earlier. I enjoyed the old show, but I think the new show is a little more slick, but he seems a whole lot happier.

Do you miss not being on the show?
I never took the thing for granted. I never knew when they were going to call. I never knew if they were going to stop calling all of a sudden. When they moved to CBS, they did have me on one time. They imported me to a building right opposite the Ed Sullivan Theater. They found an office for me and we re-created the same setup, but, of course, it was a little more contrived. I have a new job now. I'm at Workman Publishing. I started here in December.

Did you ever get a canned ham from Dave?
No. I never got a canned ham. I don't know if I should feel bad about that.

Did you ever meet him?
I only met him a couple of times. I met him that first show because they brought me into the studio to give me that man's suit of clothing. So I was sitting at his desk, next to him. We talked a little bit.

I remember it was freezing in there. Icy cold. I did go to their Christmas party when they rented out the Rockefeller skating rink. And he's a very good ice skater, I have to say

Strong or weak handshake?
Very strong. He comes across very chivalrous. Very gallant. Very gentlemanly. Much more straight, as opposed to goofy, than you would think—although he did start a food fight at the Christmas party.

Getting to Know Boutros Boutros-Gali

Boutros Boutros-Gali, also known as Pierre.

How can we talk about Dave's friends without examining the one whose name he mentions most often: Boutros Boutros-Gali. Sure we've heard all about Boutros Boutros-Gali, the man with the funny name. But how much do we know about Boutros Boutros-Gali the man? We had hoped to interview him for this book, so as to present the public with a more human image of the secretary-general of the United Nations. Unfortunately, he was too busy resolving world crises in Rwanda and Bosnia to accommodate our questions, but boy did we get his press secretary in big trouble just for asking.

Among other things, we hoped to find out whether the secretary-general is aware of his frequent mentions on Dave's shows, what his own friends call him, and whether the Security Council plans to take any action on Dave's hair. Forced to do some actual research instead, here is what we found.

BOUTROS BOUTROS-GALI

Sixth secretary-general of the United Nations.
The first secretary-general from an Arab country.

Born: November 14, 1922, in Cairo, Egypt.

Education: Received law degree from University of Cairo, 1946, and diplomas in political science, economics and public law from University of Paris, 1949

Religion: Coptic Christian. The Copts descend from Christianized Egyptians who resisted Islam more than a thousand years ago. His wife was born Jewish and converted to Catholicism as a child.

Upbringing: Born into a wealthy family, he was raised in a palace with over 100 rooms. "My uncle was a pasha, a title like a lord in England," he has said. "My grandmother was thus known as Mother of Pasha."

Prior work experience: He was at President Anwar Sadat's side when he made his historic trip to Israel in 1977 and as minister of state for foreign affairs and then acting foreign minister and chief negotiator, he was instrumental in bringing about peace with Israel. "They called me the academic engineer of Arab surrender," he commented once.

He was also a professor of law and international relations at University of Cairo.

Term as secretary-general: Beginning December 3, 1991, for five years.

Languages spoken: Arabic, French, and English.

What he does for entertainment in New York, New York, the city so nice they named it twice: "I've been two years in New York and I have never been to any theater. No—I went once with Barbara Walters, but I slept after the first act."

Who he reads for guidance: Julius Caesar.

Nickname within the UN: The Pharaoh.

Nickname to friends: Pierre (which is French for Boutros). One story has it that he was first called Pierre after striking up genial relations with his Israeli colleagues during the negotiation of the Egypt-Israel peace treaty.

History of his name: His grandfather, Boutros Gali, was the first and only modern Coptic prime minister of Egypt; he was assassinated in 1910. The family integrated his first name into their last name (hence Boutros-Gali) and further honored him by naming his grandson for him (hence Boutros Boutros-Gali).

Baby it's Cold Inside

We can't talk about Dave's pals without also mentioning his new home, the recently renovated Ed Sullivan Theater. Many viewers don't realize what a daunting task it was to renovate the old theater in time for the big show's debut in September, 1993. As Dave said at the time, "I've been in there three or four times, and every time I go in there, I stay in about eight minutes, and then all you see are big clouds of asbestos. And then I have to get out. I just think it might have been easier to renovate Ed Sullivan than the theater."

In addition to the usual challenges, the renovation team had to figure out the proper way to ice the place down so Dave could keep the studio at a comfortable 54 to 57 degrees at all times. Charles McCarry served as one of the scenic designers for the design and installation of *Late Show* during the renovations. He shared with us some details about the fascinating world of air-conditioning-duct design.

Dave gleefully bags some Streisand tickets, while Barbra catches cold.

"There is a lot of air conditioning in that building. Many times more than is actually needed to simply cool the room. All this extra air-conditioning required extra ducts. And these ducts took up vast amounts of space also needed for the set and lighting for the show.

"In the end, the designers decided to make a sandwich. Just below the stage are big air-conditioning ducts, and there are others just as big overhead. The stage is completely surrounded by air-conditioning. Swallowed up in air-conditioning, in fact. The viewers don't see it, but it's there. The stage is really in the middle of a huge air-conditioner sandwich. So is the studio audience. It gets very cold in there."

Could a Guy in a Bear Suit Get Standby Tickets to See Dave's Show?

Guy in a Bear Suit limbers up before trying to get standby tickets to see Dave's show.

Guy in a Bear Suit has apparently arrived too late to even have a chance of getting standby tickets to see Dave's show.

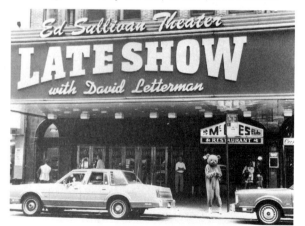

Guy in a Bear Suit outside of the Ed Sullivan Theater.

Guy in a Bear Suit rummages through Dave's trash can, in hopes of finding discarded tickets, or something to eat.

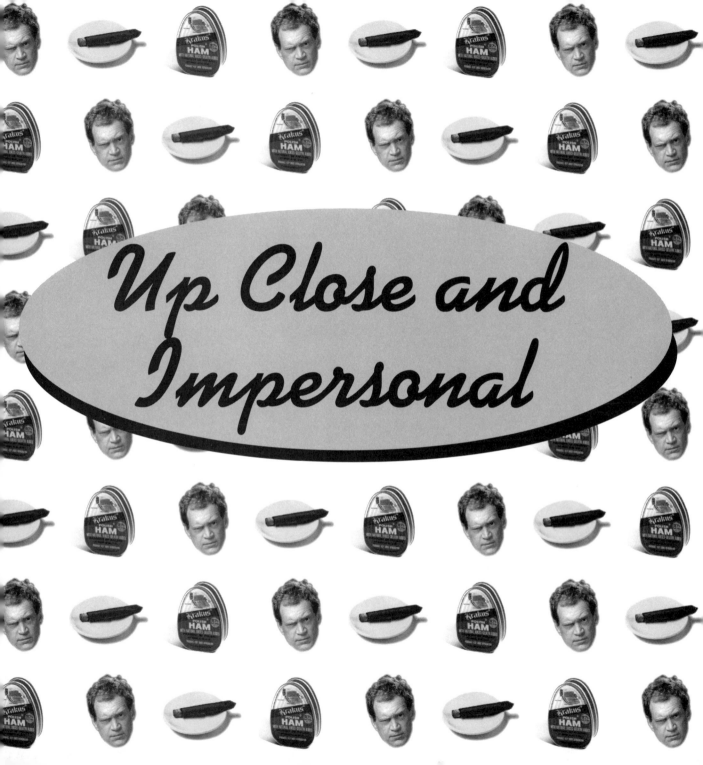

Up Close and
Impersonal

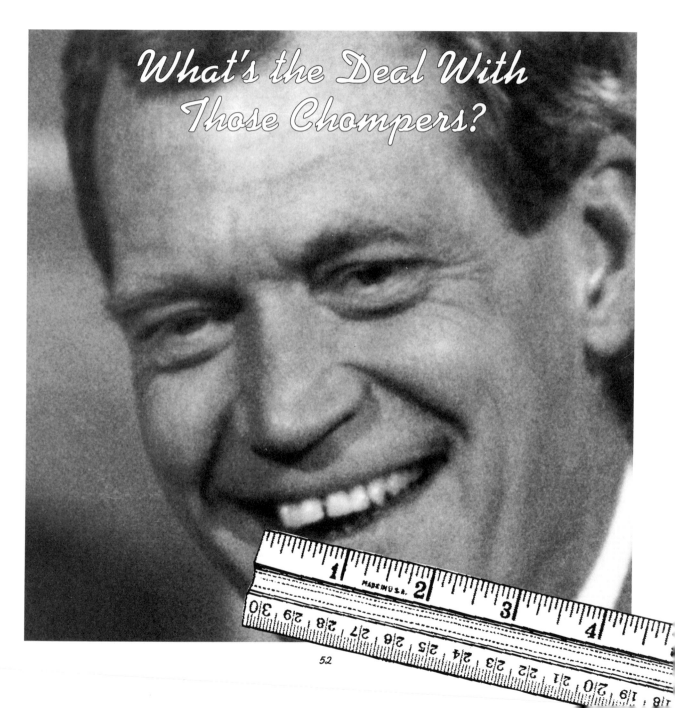

What's the Deal With Those Chompers?

Dave in 1978, when he appeared on the Mary *show, complete with a dental insert between his two front teeth. His own assessment? "I tried a spacer in front. But I have an overbite, and that amplified the problem. I looked like a duck."*

What would the Letterman smile be without these generous spaces? It almost boggles the mind to imagine such a sight. Part of Dave's appeal is that he doesn't have fancy movie star looks—he's just your goofy neighbor, dressed up and standing before the camera.

As Dave tells the tale, he didn't even know that his teeth were the slightest bit unusual until a secretary for a television special told him that he would need to get his teeth fixed. "I ran to the mirror …and honest to God, I noticed for the first time that I have these huge spaces between my two front teeth."

Like many young folks trying to get a leg up in the brutal world of Hollywood, Dave did explore the available options provided by modern dental technology. The results of his "spacer" are plain to see in his publicity picture from the *Mary* show in 1978. Why didn't this look last? As Dave said later, "when I wore [it], I couldn't speak properly. Every P just exploded into the mike."

And the whole tooth-gap issue is relatively minor, according to a column by Nelson Price in the *Indianapolis News*. "Attention always focuses on the gap in Letterman's front teeth. But the comedian said that if viewers observe closely,

Of course the front gap gets most of the attention, but a rare photo of Dave's smiling right profile clearly reveals a second, far larger gap.

they will notice he has a broken nose. The cause? A football game during Letterman's teen-age years."

But that will have to wait until we can find a good plastic surgeon. In the meantime, in the context of our mission to make Dave's life easier and more informed, we consulted with a Very Fancy Rockefeller Plaza Dentist, who reluctantly provided some fascinating advice.

How big would you estimate Dave's gap to be?
Between centrals, approximately two millimeters. Between right lateral and right canine, at least three millimeters. This is five millimeters of space in the anterior section. That is a lot of space.

How do you think it got so big?
It is probably due to the labial incline of the anteriors. It's difficult to diagnose from photographs alone. However, inclines and diastemers of this severity frequently result from tongue thrust, thumb sucking or an oral habit such as cigar smoking.

How would you counsel Dave on his gap?
The ideal treatment would be to obtain an orthodontic consult to

see if a correction can be achieved without doing any irreversible procedures. The good news is that his lip looks competent and has sufficient muscular tone to maintain the ideal position of the anterior teeth. [Great news, huh Dave?]

Many people, including Mr. Letterman, can go through life happily and successfully without doing anything in the way of treatment. In fact, most people do not perceive this as a defect until others point it out to them—just as some people are happily bald and would refuse a hair transplant if offered to them. Therefore, it all depends on the degree of neurosis that this investigation can produce with regard to stimulating Mr. Letterman to respond to the course recommended above.

How much would it cost to fix the gap?
On a superficial examination of the photographs, I believe that an orthodontic solution is preferable. If, however, the patient decides he wishes a prosthetic solution, porcelain laminates could be done on all six anterior teeth in order to spread the space among numbers of teeth. This would cost Mr. Letterman approximately $1,200 per tooth.

Any mortar, drills, or heavy machinery involved? If so, which is the most medieval?
For a prosthetic solution, diamond stones would be used to reduce a portion of the enamel on the labial surface of the tooth, extending slightly under the gum and into the interproximal areas. The edge of the tooth would be reduced slightly and later replaced with bonded porcelain.

What materials would you use?
Porcelain laminate fired at approximately 1,700

degrees in a vacuum furnace. The end product is a thin sliver of porcelain, custom-colored and shaded, which is then later bonded to the tooth surface with composite materials.

Would it change Dave's life?
That depends on him.

Would he get more dates?
Dave appears to be happy with his life right now and has an incredible self-image. I don't believe he needs any of this.

Would Dave still be able to whistle?
Not between his teeth.

Would the resulting increase in wind resistance help alleviate Dave's chronic speeding?
It would increase wind resistance if he kept his mouth open, which I don't recommend.

What other great gaps would you compare Dave's to?
They've bridged the English Channel.

Dave Says:

"I hate having my picture taken because I have a pretty good idea of what I look like and I know it's not pleasant. I'm very self-conscious about that."

Great Gaps of the World

To put things in perspective, the gap between Dave's teeth versus other famous gaps:

GAP	MEASUREMENT/APPRAISAL
Chunnel (Folkestone–Calais)	24 miles
Oliver North	Secret
David Michael Letterman	2 millimeters (estimate)
Terry Thomas	Very large
Alfred E. Neuman	Three-eighths of an inch, according to editor Nick Meglin, "but considering this is MAD magazine there's a credibility gap in that figure."
Lauren Hutton	Gaps *can* be sexy

Largest earthquake gap in California (from the Landersquake of 1992, 7.6 on the Richter scale)   26 inches

Largest gap from the 1994 North Ridge earthquake in California   16 inches

The Cumberland Gap (Kentucky, Tennessee, and Virginia)   20,274 acres

The Grand Canyon   18 miles

The Delaware Water Gap   400 feet

The Verrazano-Narrows Bridge   4,260 feet

The famous gap in Richard Nixon's tapes   1,350 feet of audiotape (estimate)

The U.S. budget gap $238.4 billion

Chaucer's Wife of Bath   "Gat toothed was she, soothly for to saye"

A Dave Hairline

EARLY 60s

LATE 60s

EARLY 70s

EARLY TO MID 70s

1978

1982

1993

Dave Says:
"By God, when they build a better hairpiece, I'll buy it!"

He's Not Just a Talk-Show Host, He Could Be a Member

Say what you want about Dave's actual hairstyle (his own longtime hairstylist, Hisao Oe of the Pierre Michel salon has said previously, "David has terrible hair. He doesn't know how to take care of it. Then he musses it all up before he goes on TV."), but there's no denying that Father Time is taking his toll on the amount of hair Dave has to work with. We wanted to be able to offer Dave some helpful suggestions, so we spoke with Sy Sperling, member and president of the Hair Club for Men

Is Dave a member of the Hair Club for Men?
No. He doesn't wear anything. His hair is thinning at this point.

Is Dave eligible?
Oh sure. He's eligible.

What do you think you could do for Dave?
I could give him better-looking hair. His hair doesn't serve him well.

Sy Sperling, president of the Hair Club for Men, before.

Sy Sperling, president of the Hair Club for Men, and client, after.

Can you tell me what his central hair problem is?
I think that he's developing a Richard Nixon hairline. Make no mistake about that. Let me make that perfectly clear.

And what would you do with that Richard Nixon hairline?
I would do away with it. I would give him a more contemporary hairstyle. I'd give him the same texture hair, but give him a nice front. Instead of it just being a patch in the front, it would flow from left to right with a nice, casual, hair-falling-on-the-forehead a little bit. We'd make him look younger and more attractive.

Get technical. What would you have to do? A weave?
We do the next level of technology. Weaving was a good system for many years, but the one problem we had with weaving, although it didn't come off, is that when somebody would run their fingers through your hair they could feel the cornrow. So we developed a system that does

Sy Sperling provided these computer images of Dave. This one shows the next stage of his hairline.

And this is where it's headed.

Here's what Dave would look like with the deluxe Hair Club treatment.

And here's Dave with the deluxe Lyle Lovett treatment.

bond the new hair to its own hair so it doesn't come off. And we're using an open mesh on the scalp so the water goes right through to your scalp and you're not smothering it. It's not like putting a toupee on the scalp. It's an open mesh that allows the scalp to breathe and whatever existing hair he has can come through.

How much would it cost?
Anywhere from $2,000 to $3,600.

Do you think the chronic cigar smoking is affecting his hairline?
No. I don't. You know, when I first got out of the air force, I attributed my thinning pate to wearing a hat all the time. But when I started to think a little bit more logically, I asked the question, Why was it that so many men who were in the air force for 30 years, career air force people, who wore that hat for 30 years had full heads of hair? So why did I lose it in four years? There

the same thing as the weaving. It gives you the same permanent effect, but you don't feel the ridges around it any more. Instead of cornrowing the hair, we're using a bonding process. We

are so many men who kept their hair after 30 years in the air force. And the answer finally came down to, maybe I lost it because I had a genetic predisposition to hair loss.

Dave's Duds

Ever since making the big move to CBS, Dave has displayed startling sartorial improvement. But trying to get the details on who fashions Dave's duds is harder than breaking into Fort Knox. If you want to know where they get the bear suit it's not too hard, but Dave's fancy new pants are another thing altogether. And so we leave you with a few fashion remarks, one from Old Dave and one from New Dave.

SLOPPY OLD DAVE SAYS:

"I have trouble there. I have two very nice people who help me with the clothing and they pick it out and they make sure that it looks nice and so forth. But the real problem is me. I just don't know what you ought to be wearing."

SNAPPY NEW DAVE SAYS:

"We did know that CBS spent a lot of money on the show. It was going to be 11:30. We were going to have a larger audience. We had to at least make it look like they were getting their money's worth from it.

"Also, from a practical side, I got so tired of, Do these pants go with this jacket? Does this tie? And now you pretty much know the jacket and pants are going to go together. That's kind of a given. So it limited the decision-making ordeal."

Let's Learn About Indiana

Dave's from there, and his Mom still lives there, so Indiana must be a fine state. But just what goes on there? We wanted to know more. For those of you who don't live within easy traveling distance of Indianapolis, Indiana, here is a little taste of what you're missing.

INDIANAPOLIS

Already the country's 12th largest city, Indianapolis is predicted to grow faster over the next five years than any other city in the Midwest. As the capital of Indiana, Indianapolis is the nation's most centrally located city to the top 100 U.S. markets. Perhaps that explains why, as the city's 1994

brochure proudly notes, "Long recognized for its progressive alliance between the public and private sectors, Indianapolis has blossomed, or better yet, exploded, into a thriving economic force. A force that was hailed as an economic 'pit bull.'"

That's right, economic pit bull. But we're figuring you folks at home aren't just interested in economics. You want some of the city that gave us Dave.

A breathtaking shot of bustling downtown Indianapolis.

62

The same brochure tells us that "today, Indianapolis is hailed as one of the major sporting capitals in the world." You'll find the Indianapolis Motor Speedway—a favorite hangout of Dave's—as well as the Hoosier Dome, Bush Stadium (home to the Indianapolis Indians, the Cincinnati Reds' farm team and winner of several AAA championships, as well as the location for the movie *Eight Men Out*), the Major Taylor Velodrome and

Lake Sullivan BMX Track, and Eagle Creek Park, offering the only sanctioned international regatta course in the United States.

Now, what are some of the other major attractions and benefits of a town like Indianapolis? Here are some additional selections from the brochure that explains it all.

Eiteljorg Museum of American Indian and Western Art
500 West Washington Street
Indianapolis' newest museum is a piece of art in and of itself. The $14 million adobe-style edifice graces downtown Indianapolis with its dusty Southwestern facade and is dedicated to the preservation and interpretation of the history of the American frontier. The museum features a $40 million collection of paintings, bronzes, pottery, basketry, and clothing from the 19th century to the present.

Beef and Boards Dinner Theatre
9301 North Michigan Road
Serving up prominent Broadway productions and highly touted concerts for more than 20 seasons, this dinner the-

ater's menu offers B.B. King, vaudeville, comedy, and other tasty morsels of sensory and culinary delights.

Indianapolis City Center, Pan Am Plaza
210 South Capitol Avenue
Whether you're looking for information about the city's history, landmarks, dining, multicultural events, or whatever, there's no better source than the Indianapolis City Center. A detailed "interactive" model of the city literally high-

THE INDIANA STATE BIRD

The cardinal, or red bird, was designated as the state bird by the Indiana General Assembly on March 9, 1933. The male bird is red with black markings and has a bright, cheery song that is heard in Indiana year-round.

lights geographic localities, landmarks, and roadways. High-tech multimedia presentations showcase some of the city's finer points, and more than 300 brochures offer both visitors and residents countless options and tidbits of information.

Broad Ripple Village
(near Dave's childhood home)
Concentrated in the Broad Ripple Neighborhood on the city's Northside lies a conglomeration of nightclubs, art galleries, sidewalk cafes, boutiques, pubs, and ethnic restaurants. It has a quintessential quaintness and is a haven for ducks.

Crown Hill Cemetery
Surrounded by one of the longest (three miles), continuous brick-masonry fences in the world, this stirring sweep of land is the nation's fourth-largest cemetery and the final home to poet James Whtcomb Riley, President Benjamin Harrison, gangster John Dillinger, and 170,000 others.

Benjamin Harrison Home
1230 North Delaware
This vast, 16-room Italianate mansion is the former residence of America's 23rd president and has been carefully restored to its 1800s appearance with original Victorian furnishings and political mementos.

Madame Walker Urban Life Center
617 Indiana Avenue
Built as a tribute to America's first, self-made African-American female millionaire, this four-story facility, now listed in the National Register of Historic Places, has been the focal point for Indianapolis's African-American cultural scene.

Murat Temple
510 N. New Jersey Street
The largest of the 190 shrine temples in the world, the Murat Temple is modeled after an Islamic mosque and features an Egyptian room with decor resembling the tomb of King Tutankhamen. The theater is also the birthplace of the Shrine Circus.

Scottish Rite Cathedral
650 North Meridian Street
Declared "one of the seven most

THE INDIANA STATE CAPITOL

was moved to Indianapolis in 1825 from Corydon. The capitol was built on its present site in 1835. It was demolished in 1878 to make way for the present Capitol Building, completed in 1888.

beautiful buildings in the world" by the International Association of Architects, this Tudor Gothic–style temple is the largest Scottish rite cathedral in the world. Highlights include a 7,500-pipe organ, a 54-bell carillon, a 200-light crystal chandelier, and intricate, handcrafted wood paneling.

THE INDIANA STATE FLOWER

The peony was adopted as the official state flower by the Indiana General Assembly in 1957. It blooms in a variety of colors, in single and double form. The zinnia had been the state flower from 1931 until 1957.

BUT WHAT ABOUT THE HARD SATISTICS?

Average temperatures (1871–1991)

	DAILY HIGH	DAILY LOW
January	34.2	17.8
April	63.1	41.7
July	85.2	64.9
October	66.1	43.4

Source: National Oceanic and Atmospheric Administration.

Some quick calculations based on these figures produce an average mean temperature of 52 degrees, which could explain Dave's penchant for keeping his studio at a nippy 54 to 57 degrees year-round.

Population, city of

Indianapolis	797,159
Indianapolis metroplitan area	1,249,822
Median age	32.3 years

Population segments

White	77.1%
African-American	21.2
Hispanic	1.1
American Indian	.02

Indianapolis has the 16th largest African-American community in the nation and the sixth-largest in the Midwest.

Source: 1990 Census

Cost of Living

Boston, MA	136.8
Washington, DC	134.2
Los Angeles, CA	130.5
Philadelphia, PA	128.6
Cleveland, OH	111.5
Portland, OR	109.4
Denver, CO	107.1
Minneapolis, MN	106.6
Peoria, IL	106.1
Cincinnati, OH	105.1
Las Vegas, NV	105.0
Charleston, VA	104.3
Dallas, TX	102.8
Phoenix, AZ	101.2
Atlanta, GA	99.6
Indianapolis, IN	**96.7**

Source: American Chamber of Commerce Researchers Association

THE INDIANA STATE TREE

The tulip tree, also known as the yellow poplar, was adopted as the official state tree by an act of the Indiana General Assembly on March 3, 1931. Monarch of the forests that covered most of Indiana in pioneer days, the tulip tree has since become comparatively rare. The lovely bell-shaped, greenish-yellow flowers appear in May or June.

Happy Hoosiers Forever

Indiana has been home to scores of other very famous and accomplished people besides Dave. Here is a partial list:

Name	Occupation	Area
Claude Akins	Actor	Bedford
Richard Allen	Writer	Indiana Univ.
David Anspaugh	Director	
Howard Ashman	Writer	
Julia Barr	Actress	Purdue Univ.
Anne Baxter	Actress	
Gary Bettenhausen	Race car driver	
Polly Bergen	Actress	
James Best	Actor	Corydon
Larry Bird	Basketball player	French Lick/ Indiana State
Bill Blass	Clothing Designer	Fort Wayne
Monte Blue	Actor	Indianapolis
Frank Borman	Astronaut	
Avery Brooks	Actor	Gary
Hoagy Carmichael	Composer	Bloomington
Poncho Carter	Race car driver	
David Chambers	Writer	
Scatman Crothers	Actor	
Jim Davis	Cartoonist	Fairmount
James Dean	Actor	Fairmount
Julia McWhirter	Comedienne	Dees
Joyce Dewitt	Actress	Speedway
John Dillinger	Gangster	Mooresville
Gloria Dorson	Actress	
Paul Dresser	Composer of state song	Fairbanks
Irene Dunne	Actress	
Bianca Ferguson	Actress	
Janie Fricke	Musician/singer	South Whitley
Crystal Gayle	Musician/singer	Wabash
Will Geer	Actor	Evansville
Bob Griese	Football player	Evansville
Ron Glass	Actor	Evansville
Virgil Grissom	Astronaut	Mitchell
Halston	Clothing designer	Evansville/Indiana Univ.
Phil Harris	Comedian	Linton
Elwood Haynes	Auto inventor	Kokomo
Florence Henderson	Actress/singer	Dale
Alex Karras	Actor/ Football player	
The Jacksons: Jackie, Janet, Jermaine, LaToya, Marlon, Michael, Randy, Tito	Musicians/singers	Gary
Dean Jagger	Actor	
John Jakes	Writer	
Emmet Kelly, Jr.	Clown	
Ken Kercheval	Actor/popcorn manufacturer	
Terry Lester	Actor	Indianapolis
The Letterman	Musicians	
Carole Lombard	Actress	
Shelly Long	Actress	Fort Wayne
Peter Lupus	Actor	
Marjorie Mann	Actress	
Kristina Malandro	Actress	
Karl Malden	Actor	Gary
Don Mattingly	Baseball player	Evansville
John Cougar Mellencamp	Musician/singer	Seymour
George McGinnis	Basketball player	Indianapolis
John McGreevey	Writer	
Steve McQueen	Actor	
Tom Moore	Director	West Lafayette
Betsy Palmer	Actress	East Chicago
Sandi Patti	Musician	Anderson
Jane Pauley	Anchorwoman	Indianapolis
Angelo Pizzo	Writer	
Sydney Pollack	Director	Lafayette
Dick Powell	Actor/singer	
Sara Purcell	Talk-show host	
Ernie Pyle	Journalist	Dana
J. Danforth Quayle	Vice-President of the United States	Huntington
Orville Redenbacher	Popcorn manufacturer	Valaparaiso/ Purdue Univ.
James Whitcomb Riley	Writer	Greenfield
Oscar Robertson	Basketball player	Indianapolis
David Lee Roth	Musician	
Wilma Rudolph	Track star	
Bob Shanks	Writer	Lebanon
Marilyn Sharp		
Herb Shriner	Comedian	Angola
Wil Shriner	Comedian	Angola
Kin Shriner	Actor	Angola
Red Skelton	Comedian	Vincennes
Henry Lee Summer	Musician	Brazil
Booth Tarkington	Writer	
Meshach Taylor	Actor	
Steve Tesich	Writer	
Twyla Tharp	Choreographer	
Forrest Tucker	Actor	Plainfield
Kurt Vonnegut	Writer	Indianapolis
Dan Wakefield	Writer	Indianapolis
Michael Warren	Actor	
Clifton Webb	Actor	
Jessamyn West	Writer	
Robert Wise	Director	Winchester
Joanne Worley	Comedienne	
Dick York	Actor	
Fuzzy Zoeller	Golfer	New Albany

Dave's Stars

What's in this star's stars? We brought in an expert, *Cosmopolitan* astrologer Allegra Quince, to read the skies above Dave. This clock-like wheel shown is a natal chart, a two-dimensional depiction of the positions of the planets within the solar system when Dave was born. The nine o'clock position, or ascendant, shows what was coming over the horizon when Dave gave his first cry; the 12 o'clock position indicates what was due north.

Because the wheel, like the sky, changes every few minutes, exactitude is fairly important in astrology. Sadly, the Indianapolis Bureau of Vital Statistics would not release Dave's birth certificate to us. The estimated time of birth was supplied by a *Late Show* intern whom we will call Madame C. All the planets remain in the same signs if the Madame C. time happens to be wrong, but they take different spots along the wheel.

Why is Dave so funny?
Jupiter on the ascendant means Dave was born to make the world a happier place. Moon in Capricorn means the joke is one of the few ways Dave can relate to other human beings.

Why is Dave a star?
The same Saturn and Pluto that make Dave so desperate for public acclaim form supporting angles to both his Sun and his Mars, so Dave's best willpower and energy help him out here. Jupiter on the ascendant brings ridiculously good luck, and the Capricorn Moon pitches in the always helpful ruthless drive.

Why isn't Dave married?
Blame Venus in Pisces—the squiggle that makes him such a sweet, sappy lover—at a hard angle to Uranus. Constant shake-ups, explosive arguments, and sudden, inexplicable changes of heart characterize Dave's relationships. Also, Uranus in the marriage house makes for at least one divorce. Nevertheless, his North Node—his destiny— sits there, too, so Dave won't really be happy until he is again wedded. According to this chart, the last week in June 2000 is a good bet for Dave's nuptials.

Why do insane women love Dave?
For one, Dave likes them too. Venus in Pisces gives Dave a weak spot for anyone with a problem, while the angle from Uranus adds moonlight madness to the equation. He'll certainly never be completely free of the crazies.

NEPTUNE IN LIBRA, RETROGRADE

The dreamy sea god was doing the backstroke when Dave was born, saddling him with a brutal cynicism toward things Libran—particularly the ideals of justice and marriage. This is simply a pose, so no one knows he's really a mushy old guy who'd rather be talking about truth and relationships all the time. This placement also indicates a deep appreciation of music's healing qualities. Go tell Paul.

JUPITER IN SCORPIO, RETROGRADE AND ASCENDING

The happy god of expansion at the ascendant makes Dave naturally sophisticated and fortunate. Because Jupiter was bounding backward in the sign of sex and death when Dave was born, Dave's affability is backed up by a wicked sensuality, and he's a Class A lover. The paranoia that's part of this package only gets directed toward his lovers or those who have power over his career. (Jupiter in Scorpio doesn't mess around with small potatoes.) Finally, Dave harbors a secret attraction for astrology. Come on out of the occult closet, honey.

MOON IN CAPRICORN

How do you spell piranha? Astrologers don't call this the Hitler Moon for nothing—if Dave is smiling at you, he probably wants something. Contract renewal time is especially tough, since Dave needs control the way the rest of us need food and water. To be fair, Abe Lincoln shared this moon, and it can indicate a wry wit, a real concern for human rights, and scathing self-criticism. As well as the aforementioned lust to run the world.

SATURN AND PLUTO IN LEO

Fish much? Dave needs flattery, and lots of it. The god of limits and the lord of death hanging out in the sign of the performer gives Dave a love-hate relationship with fame. He must have it; it'll never be enough. Here also is the childishness so prevalent in Dave's chart. Pluto in Leo makes Dave the eternal rakish lad, but Saturn nearby means Dave is bitter and resentful about childishness in himself and others. Hence the famous irony. P.S. Dave suspects he's born of royalty. Don't be the one to tell him he's not.

URANUS IN GEMINI

Dave's genius lies in information exchange; he can't abide boredom, and he is a secret champion of freethinkers and anarchists everywhere. The quicker the message gets sent, the happier Dave is. He should go on-line.

NORTH NODE IN GEMINI

Not an actual planet or star but a point arrived at through a complex geometric process, the North Node shows Dave's best shot at fulfilling his karma and avoiding the mean kids at the end of the block. Big news: Dave should be communicating for a living.

SUN IN ARIES

Mr. Personality perks up for a fight and feels sexy when danger is in the air. But it's his slightly awkward, slaphappy boyishness that nabs the victory. Sure, Dave is a fine fighter, but he coasts best on his rakish charm, a charm that's in bloom long after he—or anything about him—should be blooming at all. The downside? Aries men are the astrological captains of denial—and it ain't just a river in Egypt. If Dave believes the sky is green, you might show him color maps, opinion polls, paint-by-number kits. Piddling facts don't trouble Dave. Dave will not change course.

MARS IN ARIES

With the god of war in the sign of the Ram, Dave is a great connoisseur of recklessness, speed, pin-up girls, and everything else adolescent boys love. Yet where honor is concerned, Dave is the fabled knight in shining armor. (And doesn't he look cute when gearing up for a duel?) Deep down, Dave wishes he was a role model for the millions.

MERCURY IN PISCES

Dave's not really reading off those cue cards—the messenger god parked in Pisces gives him a photographic memory as well as an uncanny ability to say what people want—or don't want—to hear. The easy angle to Jupiter makes Dave flat-out brilliant, deftly maneuvering from small, inconsequential details to the big picture and back again. Finally, Mercury next door to Mars bestows a flair for verbal violence.

VENUS IN PISCES

Sure, Dave endures long periods of monkish isolation while dreaming of The Perfect One. But once he gets her, he's one of the best lovers in the zodiac—romantic, playful, devoted. Dave's fave love game is domination-submission, and Dave really wants to be dominated though he'd never admit it (too much fire in the chart). This placement also means Dave can play the victim to excellent advantage. If he's feeling sorry for himself, you will too.

David Letterman
April 12, 1947

Why does Dave bring his mother to work?
Psychological astrologers write whole books on charts like Dave's. They say the Moon in Capricorn harkens back to a power-hungry mom who fed her kid ambition instead of TLC. They say she is the reason Dave has gone to such lengths to host a network show; they say she is the reason he'll strive for ever greater control. It could also be that she's a good gag.

Would Dave make a good leader of a drug-related sex cult?
As a matter of fact, the Aries Sun and Capricorn Moon can turn audiences into lemmings at the drop of a hat. And with the kinky opposition between Mars and Neptune, Dave would make an excellent leader of a drug-related sex cult.

Can I expect Dave to do any cooking or house-keeping for me?
Dream on. Dave's chart is pretty well balanced, but there's a black hole where the nurturing function should be. You, however, are more than welcome to cook and clean for him.

Could this astrology stuff help Dave with his traffic tickets?
Yes! With an astrologically attuned judge, the Mars argument is indispensable. Mars in Aries boys are congenitally unable to refrain from speeding. If Dave plays the victim of his planets—and Venus in Pisces will help here—the court might well take pity.

How can a change of just one hour make such a difference in a guy's life?
While the late-night negotiations were going on, Dave was getting the assault of a lifetime from

the sky. In 1991 and 1992, Uranus and Neptune joined forces to beat up Dave's natal Sun and Moon from opposite ends, while Pluto took a mean left hook at his Saturn. Sure, he's happy because of the time change, but he's mostly relieved to have made it out of the astrological woods. Dave won't have another battle like that until 2014, when he'll probably own a couple networks.

What can Dave do if he is feeling down?
Above all, Dave should not bottle up his feelings—onstage or at home. If Dave isn't angry about some person, place, or thing, that means his scathing self-criticism has worked, and he's too depressed to care about anything. For a quick pick-Dave-up, tell him how sexy he is—he does not have any idea.

What is Dave's major astro-lesson for this lifetime?
Dave must learn to express his inner self while in performance. Irony has been a fine defense to date, but he can't hide from destiny forever. One day Dave will be spilling his guts on *Oprah*, just like everybody else.

Could a Guy in a Bear Suit Get Passport Photos at Rock America?

Guy in a Bear Suit poses with Sirajul. Everything is taken care of.

Say, "Honey."

Yes, a Guy in a Bear Suit can get passport photos at Rock America. But what did he really expect for six dollars?

Fast Cars and Slow Cigars: Extracurricular Dave

Get Your Tickets Here

Dave jokes a lot about his ongoing friendship with the Connecticut State Troopers. We thought it would be fun to have a look at his actual speeding tickets. And boy, did we hit the mother lode: seven beauties from our friends in Connecticut, and another three from the New York State Police in Westchester.

We also analyzed the tickets to see what we could learn about Dave's habits, and there are a number of things worth noting. The first is that the Dave hasn't actually been pulled over in Connecticut since the end of

1988. His most recent speeding violation was in New York on the Hutchinson River Parkway, near Harrison. And speeding isn't Dave's only weakness: Three times Dave was cited for illegally using a radar detector (a lot of good it did), twice he was written up for not having a Connecticut driver's license even though he was a resident (he still carried a California license), and twice he didn't have his license at all.

By his own admission, Dave is now somewhat of a reformed man. He recently said, "I lost my license about six years ago for speeding, and since then I've tried to be more prudent

about it. More vigilant." And indeed, last fall's lapse was his first in just over three years. We're glad Dave's trying to be more careful, since, as he noted in another interview, "I busted my neck twice in car accidents." Here's hoping the following tickets remain souvenirs of Old Dave.

SHRINKING DAVE

What's with Dave's penchant for owning fast cars and chronically violating the speed limit?
Dave likes to push the envelope. He's not in a rush, it's just that his idle speed is 4,000 rpm. Unless he is in the red line, he feels stalled. He doesn't feel alive until he feels a bit of danger, but unlike people who have no control, he likes to play off between the clutch and the gas pedal. Because he likes the feeling of being in control at all times, he'll slow down by downshifting, rather than using his brakes. His favorite road contour is probably a banked curve.

Most normal people, having been stopped within three miles of their home more than once, would exercise a little caution when they get close to home. What's Dave's problem?
He's so eager to get home that he doesn't pay proper attention. He wants to get home to a place of safety. Why is he so eager to get home? The question is, What is he running from? He lives on that edge of pushing too far, so he eagerly wants to try and find his safety zone—which means getting home.

LIFE IN THE FAST LANE

Dave's average increment above the speed limit	**21 m.p.h.**
Dave's average fine (Connecticut only)	**$121**
Number of times Dave was stopped in a car registered to NBC	**3**
Most recent time Dave was stopped in a car registered to NBC	**September 13, 1993**
Number of times Dave refused to sign his ticket	**4**
Speed Dave was clocked at on his very own street (a bucolic 25 mph zone)	**55 mph**
Number of different routes from the Merritt Parkway to his house on which Dave was ticketed	**3**
Time of day Dave was stopped for all of his tickets	**10:30 P.M. to 2:30 A.M.**
Fastest Dave's ever admitted to driving	**150 mph, in a rented Porsche Carrera Cabriolet convertible, on the autobahn**
Number of times Dave refused to sign his tickets	**4**
Number of times Dave signed his tickets, "All my best, David Letterman"	**1**

Dave was most recently nabbed for speeding in a sleek Dodge Stealth, registered to NBC.

Cars Dave was stopped in:

Jeep

GMC (two-door)

Chevy

Pontiac two-door (twice)

Porsche (twice)

Ferrari

Dodge Stealth

Dave in a Porsche, just one of his many cars. (He was caught speeding twice in one of these babies.)

Cabin Fever

fter years of success on the tube, Dave finally made his major motion picture debut earlier this year, in Chris Elliott's *Cabin Boy*. Since a lot of Dave's fans probably missed the picture—with a total box-office gross of just under $3.5 million after a six-week run, most Americans missed it— we compiled some essential facts and a selection of reviews to give you a sense of Dave's inaugural performance. Dave is not billed for the performance, in which he plays an old sea salt named Earl Hofert.

Why did it take so long for Dave to find his way to the big screen? Back in the late eighties when the television writers went on strike, Dave struck a movie production deal, through his company Cardboard Shoe, with the nice folks at Disney (the same company that made *Cabin Boy*). At the time he commented to *The Washington Post*, "The movie deal, yeah. I'm going to get out there and make bad movies. That's what we need, more of those six-dollar bombs. Actually, at the end of the contract period, if nothing has happened, I can give the money back to Disney. This is a 'movie deal' in the loosest interpretation of the phrase. At the meetings they don't say anything. There's some talk of me doing the kind of thing Buddy Ebsen used to do...At which period of his career? I don't really know. I go to those meetings, but I don't listen to anything."

But nothing ever came of the deal, prompting Dave to remark, "It just seemed unrealistic to believe that I was going to star in a movie. So we settled up the contract. They needed the cash. They were working on this Euro Disney thing and needed a little seed money. I did what I could."

But back to the business of *Cabin Boy*. It's worth bearing in mind that Elliott himself said to one journalist, "It's such an odd, quirky, bizarre film that it doesn't really fit in with the Hollywood mainstream of what movies really are." So true. Did Dave have the crystal ball out when he once noted, "I'm really confident that one day I'll make a really bad movie. It will cost about $20 million, and many people who appear in the film with me will never work again." Only time will tell.

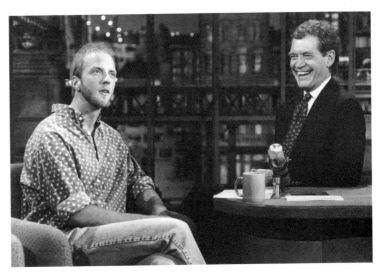

The Reviews Are In

An unmitigated disaster.
Newsday

Cabin Boy is a real shipwreck of a movie.
Los Angeles Daily News

Chewing on a cigar stub and looking more like Buddy Ebsen than ever, the gap-toothed comedian pops up near the start of the film as an old salt who perversely gives the hapless Nathanial a bum steer. "Oh man oh man, do I hate them fancy lads!" exclaims Letterman, who may, in time, come to think of *Cabin Boy* as a Stupid Human Trick that went on far too long.
The Orlando Sentinel

Not even fish-stick kitties, purple lightning, David Letterman or Charky (half-man, half-shark) can throw a lifesaver to this one.
St. Petersburg Times

A film so devoid of virtue, so want of wit and so desperate for imagination, a movie so bottomless in its craftlessness that it makes *Ishtar* seem like the height of movie making.
The Buffalo News

Cabin Boy latches onto a monotonously deadpan level of humor like a rabid barnacle and hardly ever rises above it. A certain gap-toothed TV host braves a cameo as a taunting sock-monkey salesman. "Man, oh man, do I hate those fancy lads" he grouses. Man oh, man, we know what he means.
USA Today

Letterman appears in only one brief scene, looking surprisingly small.
Chicago Tribune

If Jerry Lewis came from the fifth dimension and had Velveeta for brains, he might have made *Cabin Boy*, a comedy that's sure to amuse people who laugh when no one else in the tri-state area does.
The Arizona Republic

It's possible to watch 90 minutes of this comedy without cracking a smile. Letterman has a cameo in *Cabin Boy* and provides the only two minutes worth pulling from the wreckage. Letterman's wild grin and anarchic eyebrow-raising are a whole new experience on the big screen, and his brief appearance here is enough to make you wonder about his possibilities as a film star.
San Francisco Chronicle

Letterman appears barely disguised as a cigar-smoking old salt who is also selling monkey puppets. Ah! Typecasting! Clearly enjoying the banter with his protégé, the grinning CBS star taunts the bewigged Nathanial by saying, "You remind me of my niece Susie. Lovely girl. She's a dietitian." That exchange is one of the few funny ones in this story, which quickly sinks into a series of not-too-amusing bits of idiocy aboard the scow.
Chicago Sun-Times

The only inspired bit in *Cabin Boy* comes courtesy of old pal Letterman, who is high-energy hilarious as a fast-talking, stuffed-monkey salesman. Alas, it's only about a two-minute cameo, and it's near the beginning of the movie. Becalmed audiences, drifting through the remaining hour and a quarter, will recall those precious moments fondly.
The San Diego Union-Tribune

David Letterman makes a *Cabin Boy* cameo that's as witless as everything else in the film.
Sacramento Bee

Call this one *The Nightmare After Christmas*. Obnoxious, snide and pointless, this ill-fated spoof carries the bonus of being as crude and gamy as the hold of an old fishing barge. Still, that aroma probably won't linger, as this fish figures to sail out of theaters quickly. Even old pal Dave Letterman, listed in the credits as Earl Hofert, turns up briefly and, indicative of the general malaise, draws barely a chuckle.
Variety

Letterman was about the funniest thing in the movie. Best exchange: Elliott, as a prissy rich kid, remarks that he's famished, and Letterman who performed in Mary Tyler Moore's short-lived variety show responds, "Well, why wouldn't you be? Big girls have big appetites."

The Record

A perfect unbilled cameo by Letterman that's worth the price of admission. It's basically downhill from there.

Seattle Times

Elliott, who won four Emmys as a writer for David Letterman, has cast Big Dave in a hilarious film cameo as a salty old dog with a weird sense of humor. "He's my greatest supporter," says Elliott, "and everything leads back to him. Originally, we were going to have him in drag, but then Adam wrote the part in for him."

The Buffalo News

Another cross-demographic picture that seems destined to bypass all demographics. David Letterman pops up for a couple of unbilled minutes as a denizen of the dockside village Elliott visits pre-voyage, and he cackles his way through the entire scene, patronizing the befuddled star as hilariously as he used to in the NBC days of yore. This marks the first screen work Disney has gotten out of the talk-show host since making that multimillion-dollar movie deal with him some years back; he so lights up the screen in his brief time he

makes you hope they talk him into a Letterman-and-Elliott feature, though breath-holding isn't advised.

Los Angeles Times

Bizarre without being funny.

The New York Times

Stanley Kubrick, filmdom's famed perfectionist, would probably throw up his hands in disgust. David O. Selznick and all those late, great movie makers who labored over the minutest details might rise from the dead to destroy the prints. Federico Fellini now, HE might have liked Chris Elliott's eccentric new *Cabin Boy*.

The Record

On the Other Hand...

Three Stars. A minor screwball delight, this burlesque of *Captains Courageous* indulges Arabian Nights flights of fantasy, though undeniably inconsistent and often downright botched. But when it's funny, you know you've found something impishly fresh.

The Washington Times

From its first moment, *Cabin Boy* dispenses with any rules of rationality or constancy; in this world, it makes perfect sense that Nathanial goes from riding in a limousine to walking into a 17th-century fishing

village, or that he and his piratelike comrades sail their ancient vessel into a surreal region of flying cupcakes, shark men and anthropomorphic icebergs. It is this fearless willingness to not be bound by any restrictions, to go in any direction the comic momentum carries it, to dare to be stupid and weird, that drives *Cabin Boy* and creates such memorable moments as Nathanial scrubbing the deck with his beard or serving up his specialty, fishstick-kitties, to the hungry crew.

San Francisco Examiner

Cabin Boy is so unabashedly stupid, it's smart. Described by Elliott on Letterman's show as a cross between *Captains Courageous* and *The Seventh Voyage of Sinbad* (Letterman: "Do people want that?" Elliott: "Ask me if I care"). *Cabin Boy* is the story of Nathanial Mayweather, an insufferably snide, lazy, manipulative, fey, egotistical rich kid being prepped for life as a Fancy Lad at the Stephenwood Finishing School for Young Men. Some have already anointed Beavis and Butthead as the Jerry Lewis of the '90s, but Elliott has achieved something finer. He's the thinking person's idiot.

The Dallas Morning News

Cabin Boy, which opened here yesterday, contains about enough laugh-out-loud sight gags and non sequiturs to justify what it demands of a viewer's time and money.

The Washington Post

"Where the Hell are the Singing Cats?"

This poor confused patron is, of course, in the wrong theater. To avoid any further confusion, since after all many Broadway customers are here in New York City for the first time, here are the details on tickets for *Cats*. The show is at the Winter Garden Theater at 50th Street and Broadway. Tickets range from $37.50 to $65 and are available by phone form Tele-Charge at (212) 239-6200.

We hear from a lot of folks, saying, "I've got me a fine canned ham in the pantry and I'm ready to enjoy it with friends and loved ones, but I'm embarrassed to admit that I don't know the proper way to serve and enjoy my ham." Unfortunately, in all too many otherwise fine and upstanding American homes, the art of canned ham cookery is a lost one. At the rate Dave gives these babies out, we figured a lot of people were in need of guidance. And so we canvassed some of the leading fancy chefs of our nation.

Martha Stewart's Glazed Canned Krakus Ham

Martha Stewart

Martha wants readers to make sure that they use only Krakus brand Polish canned ham for this recipe, which is her canned ham of choice. Martha's family is from Poland, which makes this ham extra-special to her.

1 12 to 14 pound precooked Krakus canned ham
1½ cups apricot jam
¾ cup grainy mustard
3 tablespoons sherry
pea vines (optional)

1. Heat oven to 300 degrees. Place ham in a foil-lined roasting pan. Bake 1½ to 2 hours.

2. In a bowl, combine jam, mustard, and sherry.

3. Remove ham from oven. Let stand for 15 minutes or until cool enough to touch. With a large, sharp knife, score the top of the ham at ½-inch intervals in a diamond pattern. Make cuts about a ½ inch deep. Spoon half the glaze over the ham.

4. Return ham to oven for 45 minutes. Spread remainder of glaze as ham begins to shine.

5. Serve warm or at room temperature. Garnish with pea vines, if desired.

Serves 16–20

Emeril Lagasse's Creole White Beans and Ham

Emeril Lagasse

In case you are lucky enough to win a canned ham from David while you are on the show, here is a recipe that will accent the flavor of the ham.

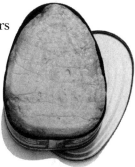

1 cup white navy beans, soaked 8 hours
2 cups water
12 ounces Dixie beer
1 cup diced ham
3 ounces Creole mustard
Salt and pepper to taste

1. Drain the soaked beans in a colander. Place in a medium-size pot and add water.

2. Simmer over medium heat for 30 minutes.

3. Add beer, ham, and mustard, and season to taste with salt and pepper. Cook 30 to 35 minutes longer until beans are soft. Set aside.

Serves four

Jasper White's Shirred Eggs à la Dave Letterman

Jasper White

Here is a simple and tasty version of ham and eggs using thin slices of canned ham. It's great for breakfast with toast or for lunch with a small salad and crusty bread. My kids even like this—I hope Dave does too!

3 tablespoons sweet butter
1 medium onion, thinly sliced
8 ounces canned ham, thinly sliced
Ground black pepper
4 large eggs
Kosher salt
2 ounces cheddar cheese, grated (white cheddar, not the orange stuff!)

1. Preheat the broiler. Set the shelf (rack) so it will be close to the bottom. For most ovens use the second shelf from the bottom.

2. Grease a square Pyrex (or other baking dish) 21 x 21 cm. (8½ inch square) with 1 tablespoon of butter.

3. Put a skillet on medium-high heat and sauté the sliced onion in 1 more tablespoon of butter. Cut the sliced ham crosswise into strips about ¾ inch wide. When the onions are lightly browned, remove the pan from the heat and mix in the ham. Season with black pepper to taste (no salt needed, yet).

4. Place the ham mixture in the baking dish. Spread evenly, then make 4 holes (kind of like nests). Crack the eggs individually and place 1 in each hole. Sprinkle the eggs with a little salt and pepper if you like, then cover the top of the dish evenly with the grated cheddar and dot with the remaining tablespoon of butter.

5. Place the dish in the oven, on a lower rack. Leave the door closed or slightly cracked. Broil for 8 to 10 minutes, depending on your oven, until the top is crusty and golden brown. Cut into 4 squares and serve at once.

Serves four

Mock Canned Ham Casserole

This being the nineties, we find that a number of people yearn for the experience of eating a canned ham, but dietary restrictions or principles preclude the use of ham in their diets. (Which is not to imply that a canned ham is anything other than a wholesome and nutritious dish.) In consideration of such special needs, we created the following recipe to fit any diet. We must warn you that this recipe is untested, and we cannot assume responsibility for how it turns out. We must also warn you that it may taste like a cross between canned ham and apple pie.

Pastry for a 2-crust 9-inch pie
36 Ritz Crackers, coarsely broken (about 1¾ cups crumbs)
2 cups water
2 teaspoons cream of tartar
2 tablespoons lemon juice
Grated rind of 1 lemon
2 tablespoons vegetable-oil spread
2 cloves garlic, diced
Pepper to taste
3 tablespoons, hot sauce
(That's right—no ham required!)

1. Preheat oven to 425 degrees.
2. Line a 9-inch pie plate with half of the rolled-out crust.
3. Put cracker crumbs inside the crust.
4. Mix water and cream of tartar and bring to a boil. Lower heat and let simmer for 10 minutes. Then add lemon juice and rind, garlic, and hot sauce. Let cool.
5. Pour liquid on top of cracker crumbs and cover with small dollops of vegetable oil spread on top. Sprinkle with pepper.
6. Roll out the remaining half of the crust and place over the top.
7. Embellish crust as desired (flutes would be nice). Make slits to allow steam to escape.
8. Bake for thirty minutes, or until golden and crisp.
9. Let cool somewhat before serving.

Dave's Sweet and Spicy Chunky Ham Salad

Chunky, chunky, chunky! That's the best way to describe this recipe, specially created in Dave's honor. We know what he likes, and here's how we're guessing he would like it.

4 sticks butter
1 liter imitation pure maple flavor syrup
2 cans pineapple
1 canned ham
½ bottle hot sauce

Cut butter, pineapple, and ham into equal sized chunks. Add syrup and hot sauce and toss lightly. Eat to extremes.

Serves one

Dave Says:
"I loves the hot sauce."

Michael McLaughlin's Nacho Mamma's Macaroni and Cheese (with Green Chiles and Canned Ham)

Given the average shelf life of several of the major ingredients, this is a good dish to serve to unexpected guests, or during a hurricane.

2 tablespoons unsalted butter or olive oil
½ pound canned ham, trimmed cubed
1 pound Velveeta processed cheese food loaf, diced
½ cup milk

½ pound dried short pasta, such as fusilli or penne, cooked until tender and drained
1 cup canned corn kernels with red and green chiles, well drained
⅓ cup chopped roasted hot green chiles, canned or thawed, well drained
2 green onions, trimmed and thinly sliced (optional)
¼ cup finely crushed corn tortilla chips

1. Preheat the oven to 400 degrees.

2. In a medium skillet, melt the butter. Add the canned ham and cook until lightly browned, about 7 minutes. Remove with a slotted spoon; reserve the butter.

3. In a medium saucepan combine the Velveeta and milk. Stir over low heat until smooth.

4. Butter a 6-cup casserole. In a bowl stir together the canned ham, Velveeta sauce, pasta, corn, chiles and the green onions if you are using them. Spoon into the casserole. Sprinkle the crushed tortilla chips over the casserole. Drizzle the crushed chips with 1 tablespoon of the butter from the skillet.

5. Set the casserole in the oven and bake until the cheese is bubbling and the top is lightly browned, 30 to 40 minutes. Serve hot.

Serves four

As a coauthor of *The Silver Palate Cookbook* and author of *The Back of the Box Gourmet*, Santa Fe-based food writer Michael McLaughlin walks a fine culinary line. Carrying a canned ham helps him keep his balance, and also makes a fine doorstop. He always watches Letterman; it's the only thing that makes him miss New York.

Dave's like butter, and he likes butter too.
Here's what he looks like in butter.

Life of a Yo-Yo Dieter

It's all well and good for many people to be thinking about ways to enjoy a delicious canned ham, but poor Dave has to think twice before treating himself to such a rich repast. As Dave made clear at the beginning of the new show in 1993, he has been battling his weight for some time now. From a skinny college kid, Dave ballooned by almost 50 pounds before realizing it was time to do something.

New Dave looks smashing in his current fighting trim of approximately 175 pounds and we're hoping he can continue to keep the weight off. Once again trying to make Dave's life a little easier, we consulted with Tiffany Middendorf at the Pritikin Longevity Center to see what words of advice she might have.

Dave's about 6'2" with a puny frame. What's his ideal weight?
Based upon Dave's height and frame size, his ideal weight would be between 170 and 195 pounds. How-

ever, a more precise measure of fitness require calculation of his percent body fat.

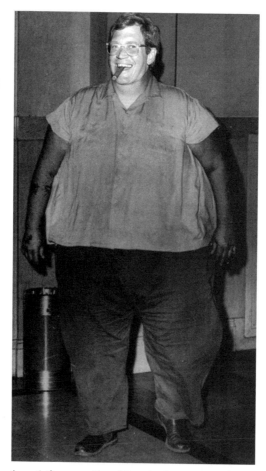

An artist's conception of Dave in the summer of 1993, before he trimmed down for the new show.

Dave weighed 153 in college. He swelled to 210 in the early nineties and now he's down to 175. Does he have that Yo-Yo syndrome?
So it would seem. Unfortunately, dieting is one of the most successful strategies for potential weight gain due to its effects upon the metabolism. It may be difficult for Dave to stay svelte if he doesn't eat well. Dave's stress level may also be an important factor to consider, as many people use food as a coping mechanism. Certain foods, particularly sweets and starchy foods, alter the brain chemistry and produce a calming effect. Over-indulgence in these foods is a form of self-medication that can ultimately result in weight gain.

What can the Pritikin Center do for Dave?
Get him off the weight roller coaster and onto the merry-

go-round. The Pritikin program combines the key elements of nutrition, exercise, and stress management to address all aspects of health, including weight loss.

Is cigar smoking an effective dieting tool?
Actually, there is nothing inherent about smoking that is an effective tool for weight control.

Why is Dave obsessed with canned ham?
Obsessive food cravings often indicate a nutrient imbalance, although this is more commonly manifested in starchy and sweet foods.

Exactly what kind of eating disorder does Dave have?
Inherently it isn't Dave with the eating disorder. His problem is equivalent to putting water into your gasoline tank. The malfunction is a result of the fuel, not the machine. Dave's problem is shared by many who are battling the ill effects of dieting. These weekend food warriors starve all week to indulge on the weekends. However, the urge to overeat becomes uncontrollable. This is no mystery to science, as we are biologically programmed to respond to a lack of food by craving increased quantities of fat and sugar.

Dave Says:

"I found in my experience that I'm always hungry. I try not to eat so much during the week—then on the weekends, once I start, I guess you'd better call the paramedics, because you'll find me face down on the kitchen floor."

DAVE'S DAY AT PRITIKIN

6:30 A.M.	Wake Up and Stretch (optional)
7:00–10:00 A.M.	Breakfast: bagel, nonfat ricotta cheese, fresh grapefruit
8:00 A.M.	Lecture: Myths and Realities of Weight Loss
9:15 A.M.	Exercise class: treadmill workout
9:45–11:30 A.M.	Morning snacks: fresh peaches, raw vegetables, vegetable soup
10:30 A.M.	Doctor's appointment
11:30 A.M.	Cooking School: Entertaining with Ease
11:30–2:00 P.M.	Lunch: Pasta marinara, whole wheat roll, fresh vegetables, salad bar, iced tea
1:00 P.M.	Workshop: Dining Out
2:00 P.M.	Low-Impact Aerobics
2:00–4:00 P.M.	Afternoon snacks: artichoke, baked potato, raw vegetables with onion dip
3:00 P.M.	Walk along the beach
5:00 P.M.	De-Stress Training
6:00–7:15 P.M.	Dinner: poached salmon, asparagus, rice pilaf or new potatoes, salad bar. Fresh berries for dessert
7:30 P.M.	Entertainment

A sample of the yummy, and healthful, food that Dave would enjoy during a stay at the Pritikin center in Miami Beach, Florida.

The Handwriting on the Wall

> MAIL TO CENTRALIZED INFRACTIONS BUREAU
> P.O. BOX 5044, Hartford, CT 06102-5044
> ANSWER DATE ➤ (Month, day, year) 12-18-88
> SIGNATURE (Person receiving complaint)
> X

For more about Dave's voluptuous loops, read below.

In our search to find out more about Dave, the man behind the mask, we submitted some handwriting samples (obtained from Dave's speeding tickets) to international handwriting expert Charles Hamilton, who has also appeared on the show with Dave. Hamilton was the first one to expose the fraudulent Hitler diaries. Here is what we learned.

Characterize Dave's handwriting.
Basically, it's a rather disorganized handwriting. It's got lots of points in the letters, which indicate high intelligence. It has a T-bar that looks more like a crow bar. This shows a very quick, alert mind and more-or-less soaring intellect.

Do you see any signs of irritation or agitation, given that he's just been stopped?
No. But I see a lot of signs of enormous impatience. He's a very impatient man. He doesn't brook delays. He doesn't tolerate people who say, "Let me think for a minute"—then he *crowns* you.

Handwriting expert Charles Hamilton.

Is there anything in his handwriting that would suggest anything about his sexuality?
I think he's quite a sexy person. He has these big, voluptuous loops. Look at 'em. My God!

Do you see any relation between this handwriting and the enormous gap between Dave's teeth?
I didn't know that there was a gap between his teeth.

What great characters in history does this autograph resemble?
David Berkowitz.

Son of Sam!?
Yes. Looks a little like his handwriting.

JumboTron, JumboFun

Viewing an enjoyable TV program like *Late Show* on your screen at home is quite pleasurable, but viewing Dave and his wacky antics on the Sony JumboTron deep in the heart of beautiful Times Square is an extra-special experience. We wanted to find out more about this marvelous invention, and the entire Sony Video 1 television broadcast. Here, direct from the good folks at Sony, is all that and more.

How it works
A JumboTron system converts analog video signals to digital data and then reconstructs the image in memory. Each frame of memory is scanned vertically onto the screen, one column at a time. This high speed repretitive process produces motion video.

Why JumboTron
The name JumboTron is basically derived from Sony's award winning trini-lite technology. The trini-lite cells that make up a JumboTron screen are actually tiny CRT devices, like a television picture tube. The term JumboTron applies to its massive size.

How jumbo it is
Pixelations: 215,424 pixels
Lines per inch: 396 vertical display lines
Electricity used: 70.22 kilowatts per hour
Dimensions: 23 feet vertical by 31 feet horizontal (713 square feet)

What it costs
A typical screen the size of Sony Video 1 JumboTron lists for approximately $3.9 million, excluding installation and control room.

How many inches is the gap in Dave's front teeth when viewed on the JumboTron
Can't answer—don't know.

The Sony JumboTron, the visual heartbeat of lovely Times Square. For just under $4 million, this could be yours (control room sold separately).

Sometimes a Cigar is Just a Cigar

Dave sure does love them cigars. He loves to have his picture taken with them, he uses them to promote weight loss, and you can often catch him sneaking a smoke in between guests on the show. We spoke with Joel Sherman, president of Nat Sherman, Inc.—justifiably known as the "Tobacconist to the World," who blew a little smoke about Dave's well-known love of cigars. As it turns out, Sherman's store has supplied Dave with cigars in the past.

Do you have any general observations about cigar smokers and any specific ones as they might apply to Mr. Letterman?
If you look at all your great leaders, all of your great athletes, all of your great successful people—and powerful people—have been cigar smokers. It's been said that if Winston Churchill hadn't smoked cigars we might all be speaking German.

Dave Says:
"I should quit. I'm smoking them like chewing gum. God help me. I love cigars."

There's John F. Kennedy; some of the more emasculated men like our current president used to smoke cigars until his wife told him to stop. I think he's a closet smoker at this point. So cigar smokers tend to be leaders of industry, leaders of government, powerful people — but all of them are fun-loving people.

What is the psychological profile of a typical cigar smoker?
Someone who is not afraid to state his or her position and express their freedom of choice. Cigar smokers tend to be courteous people who don't abuse the fact that they're smoking cigars and do it in a rather considerate fashion. They're doers and people who thrive on pressure and action.

Dave's been known to smoke Romeo and Juliettas. What does this say about his taste in cigars?
There are two kinds of Romeo and Julietta. Romeo and Julietta

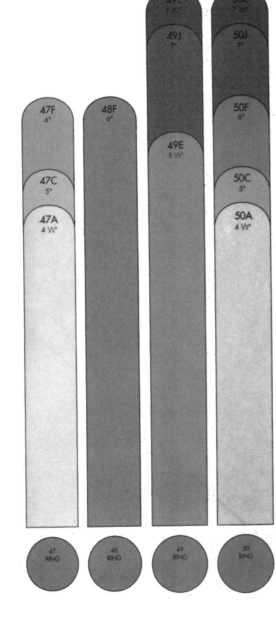

as a brand in this country is owned by different people and made in Honduras. And the Romeo and Julietta that, supposedly, if he does smoke them, and nobody knows, are Cubans—they're very different.

Which one do you think he smokes?
I'm sure if he smokes Romeo and Julietta, he smokes the Cuban. His preference is for Cuban cigars. Definitely.

Can you describe what it tastes like?
Typically the Cuban cigar is not aged or cured, so they have a very high degree of ammonia, which speaks very well for his constitution, Dave's fortitude and his strength. Most people would drop at the first puff. It speaks highly of his ability to withstand pain.

The thought and the memory of the Cuban cigar, the desire for the cigar is akin to the memory of your first love, your first great conquest, if you should call it that. As you remember it, it was wonderful, it was the most exciting thing that ever happened. If you're really truthful with yourself, it probably really wasn't that good and was something you probably hoped to improve upon in later life. So it's the memory of the forbidden fruit and the unattainable.

The right size cigar is the one that an individual likes the best, feels most comfortable with, and the one that "fits." A smoker should "wear" a good cigar. Length and ring gauge have a major effect on a cigar: The same cigar that you've just rejected, may in a different size be just what you're looking for. This chart shows a number of Sherman's popular cigar sizes. Dave's preference, a 54 (known informally as a BMF) is too large to fit on this chart. What a man.

Given that Dave has to light and then stop smoking, does he have to smoke a particularly good cigar or a particularly bad one?

The question often comes up, Can you relight a cigar? I'm sure Dave must relight a cigar many times because if it's a long segment with somebody and the camera's on him he has no choice. As long as the natural oils and tobacco are still warm and loose, you can relight it. Once they begin to crystallize after 20 minutes to a half an hour of being out, at this point the cigar will begin to taste foul and smell foul. There is no such thing as a bad cigar because it's a man's personal taste as to what he likes. If he wants a foul-tasting cigar, that's his business.

Dave is in his late forties, has no children, and is not married. Is there any connection to cigar smoking?

Probably he doesn't choose to share his cigars and guards them jealously. Margaret Ray may only be looking for some really good cigars.

Dave Says:

"Eventually I'll quit again. But I have too many things in my head now to be worrying about giving up cigars. The other thing is, if I could stop smoking cigars, I would probably gain back all my weight, and I'm fighting that daily. It's very difficult."

SHRINKING DAVE

As a professional, do you have any general observations you can share with us about cigar smokers? Any specific observations which relate to Dave?

Oh, you want me to jump to the obvious, don't you? You'd like me to be a typical Freudian jerk or asshole, right? You want me to say that he's trying to make up for lagging masculinity, don't you? That he's overcompensating for deep feelings of insecurity. That he's trying to sublimate his masturbatory impulses to holding only a cigar rather than playing with himself. Or worse his anal fixation with holding onto a thick brown cylinder rather than smearing "ca-ca" all over the place. Well, you won't get me to say those things. I think the only thing he's trying to make up for is the gap in his teeth. If it was a smaller gap he'd smoke a Tiparillo or a cigarette. If there was no gap, he'd smoke dental floss, and I'd guess it would be of the cinnamon-waxed variety.

What do you think of Dave's gap and is there any relation to cigar smoking?

There are three basic kinds of cuts in the end of a cigar. One is a guillotine or flat cut. The other is a notched V cut for opening the end of a cigar. And the third is a tooth cut. Dave is blessed with the ability to, while doing the tooth cut, do the notch cut, which is best of all. And therefore his gap is probably a great benefit developed for this purpose.

A dentist told us that thumbsucking, along with cigar smoking, might have produced or exacerbated the gap between his teeth. Please comment.

WHAT'S DAVE SMOKING?

"His fame as a television personality inhibits some of his joy as a cigar smoker. People love to come into the shop and sit in the humidor and browse and sit in the armchairs and smoke. He can't come out. He doesn't get to do his own shopping.

"He'll send his secretary in and she'll have the parameters of what he wants and we'll give her three or four humidors and she'll take them back and return the ones that he doesn't want. People buy him gifts here—we do not sell Cuban cigars; it's against the law, but we have some very similarly shaped cigars with a Cameroon wrapper. It's very full bodied, without the ammonia content. I know he smokes those.

"One of the things which is unique about Cuban cigars is they're the only cigars in the world with product totally from one country. In other words, cigars with a Cameroon wrapper have Jamaican, Dominican, Honduran, Brazilian fillers with Mexican binders. In Cuba, everything comes out of Cuba. A good cigar will take a minimum of three years from the field to the table. Dave's cigar tends to be all Cuban tobacco— much less cured, much less aged. It tends to be a very powerful cigar, very specific and pungent in taste."

—Joel Sherman

I don't know if it exacerbated the gap, but it was probably never corrected when he learned how useful it was for cutting his cigars. Some people would die for that ability not to carry around an extra piece of equipment to cut their cigars properly.

What would happen to someone less robust than Dave who smoked his cigars. What symptoms would they develop?
I don't think it's a matter of robustness or size. It's a matter of mental set and intestinal fortitude. It has to do with the ability to withstand adversity and pain.

Could a Guy in a Bear Suit Write a Book about Dave?

See inside for the answer.

441-372⅛

1961.51